THE MOST BEAUTIFUL
VILLAGES OF GREECE

MARK OTTAWAY · PHOTOGRAPHS BY HUGH PALMER

With 285 color illustrations

Thames & Hudson

Half-title

The Greek love of flowers is seen here in the village below the medieval citadel of Koroni.

Title pages

The mountain village of Ipsounda in the Peloponnese; its ancient acropolis and churches date back to the 10th century.

These pages

The port of Yialos on the island of Symi owed its original wealth to sponge-diving, and remains one of the most active and stylish harbours in the Aegean.

Copyright © 1998
Thames & Hudson Ltd, London
Text Copyright © 1998
Mark Ottaway
Photographs Copyright © 1998
Hugh Palmer

Maps by ML Design

First published in 1998 in hardcover in the United States of America by Thames & Hudson Inc., 500 Fifth Avenue, New York, New York 10110

thamesandhudsonusa.com

First paperback edition 2011

Library of Congress Catalog Card Number 97-61611

ISBN 978-0500-28930-3

Printed and bound in China by Toppan Leefung Printing Limited

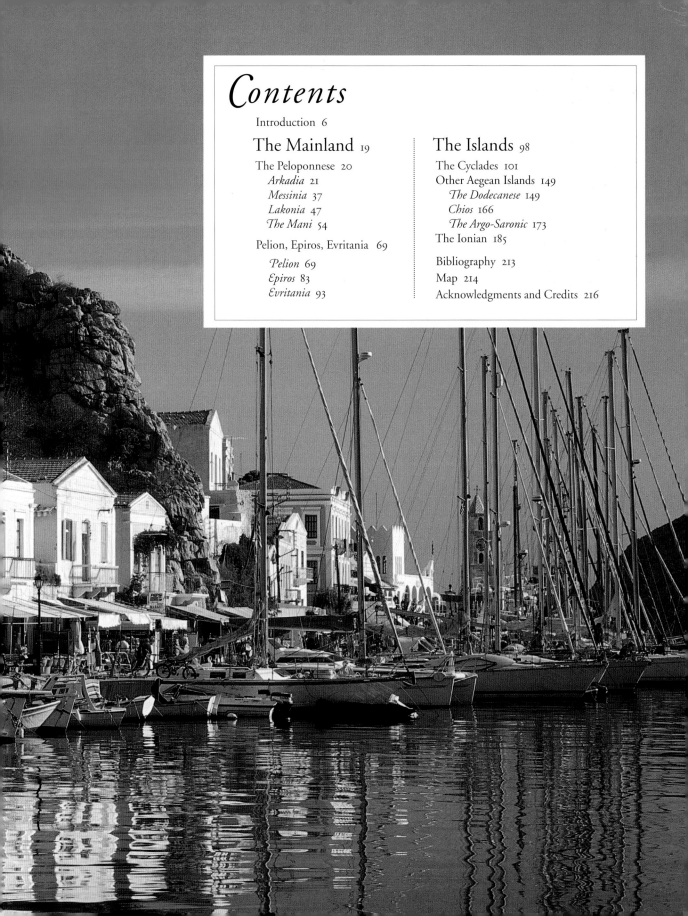

Contents

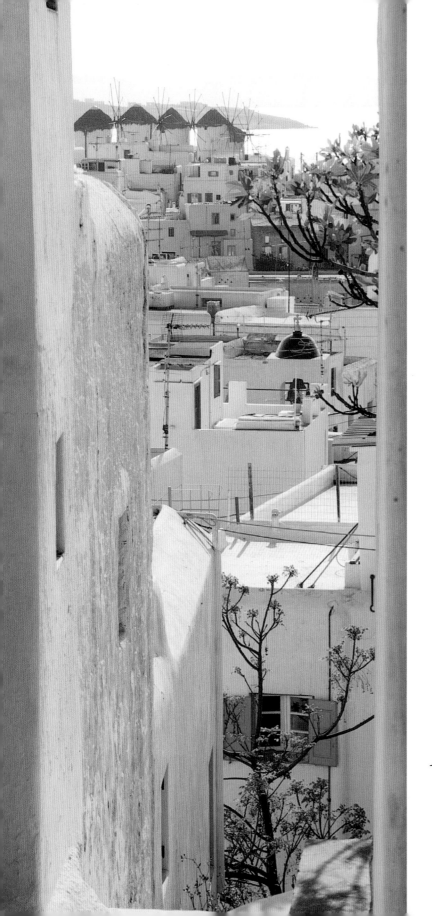

Introduction

Mykonos, one of the wonders of vernacular Cycladic architecture (left), is exactly how we expect a Greek island village to look, with white cuboid houses and windmills overlooking the harbour.

Many of the houses of Monemvassia (above) *are ripe for tasteful restoration.*

Greece is many cultural microclimates with a common theme of amazing power. Consider these facts: Greece the political entity we now know is not very old; it came into being when the Dodecanese were handed back from Italy by the British in 1947, while much of the mainland was still part of the Ottoman Empire at the turn of the century. It is a country which has never existed before: it started as a collection of bickering city states which were subsequently subsumed into greater and by no means exclusively Greek political entities from Alexander's day on, while in more recent times it has been carved up among foreign occupiers. But there has never before been a nation state called Greece.

And yet the idea of Greece, the spirit of Greekness, is one of the most durable in history. Open an Athenian newspaper today and it will include words written precisely as Homer, or those who preserved Homer's words, wrote them at the dawn of literature 3,000 years ago (and indeed 'idea' is one). And when St. John began his gospel, 'In the beginning was the Word', he penned a sentence that no Greek today is likely to have much difficulty in reading and understanding.

But it can be a mistake to draw too many expectations from the classics when approaching Greece for the first time. The rapidly dwindling band of those who have any acquaintance with them are liable to be disappointed if they land in Greece expecting daily classical resonances, though they will of course find the odd archaeological site. Speaking for myself, it was my love of Greece that inspired my interest in ancient Greece and the classics, not the other way round. There is also a tendency to overlook and underestimate the more recent Byzantine/Crusader and, for that matter, Turkish past.

The real testimony to the amazing durability of Greekness can be found in the daily lives and villages of Greece. In the language, of course, of these for so long separated people, in the teachings and influences of the Greek Orthodox church, but above all in the cafés and tavernas. They may drink *raki* and nibble pre-prandial grilled octopus in Aegean villages, while in Ionian ones both are virtually unobtainable, *ouzo* and olives being preferred, but both sets of people are undeniably Greek, of the same culture and way of life.

Much of the beauty of Greece and its islands lies in the fact that it is on the edge: not too different, but still a refreshing change. Its people are

*V*illages in the high mountains, such as Kosmas (top), made their roofs from heavy slabs of local stone. Cycladic ones, like Naxos (above), tend to be flat or gracefully vaulted, while in areas with Frankish influence, like Dimitsana (opposite), the age-old Mediterranean-wide Roman tiles prevailed.

not only Europeans, they were the first Europeans as we like to define them: the inventors of democracy and reason as a means of conducting human affairs, who in about the 6th century B.C. put off Oriental pomp and ornament in favour of a simpler and, to us, purer way.

On the other hand the place is undeniably different. It lacks many of the cultural references, landmarks or memories, even an alphabet, which might be familiar to us. Those drinks, *ouzo* and *raki*, not to mention the resinated wine, are drunk nowhere else in Europe and are (sometimes never) acquired tastes. The national music is alive and reasonably well and peculiar to our ears. Greeks don't celebrate birthdays but name days: the day of the saint who has the same name. The most important festival of their year is not Christmas but Easter. And it rarely falls on the same day as our Easter.

Greece has only recently emerged from its dark ages ('slavery' in their estimation) under foreign rulers. Though little of what held it together may have been written down, been part of Renaissance culture, or left any public monuments, in one small but very significant way its vernacular village architecture carried the torch for Greek defiance and the country that finally emerged. It is no coincidence that the now familiar and once almost universal Aegean colour scheme, white walls and blue woodwork, is the colour of the national flag. When foreign occupiers banned the flag the Greeks simply incorporated it into their houses instead.

If their country contains few tangible relics of those years, the Greeks have compensated (over-compensated the foreigner may sometimes feel) with a keen sense of history, trauma and imperilled nationhood. The Turkish presence next door is every bit as palpable and fraught for the Greeks today as for many years the Communist one was for the West.

Greek history and today's older generation at least have a tendency to lump western Europeans together as 'Franks', because it was the Franks, or more precisely the Normans, who began the pillage of Byzantium from the west which the Turks completed from the east. Other groups, Crusaders, Catalans, Genoese and Venetians joined the feeding frenzy and were sometimes referred to as 'Latins'. But for centuries what the British called 'Europeans' the Greeks called 'Franks'.

It is, perhaps, worth a brief summary of Greek history, and in particular its more recent history, to put some of this in context. The earliest Greek cultures seem to have started in the islands, with the Cycladic and Minoan civilizations (centred on the Cyclades and Crete respectively) dating as far back as 3000 B.C. The Mycenaeans, also known as the Acheans, whose ascendancy on the mainland began around 1900 B.C., seem to have absorbed many elements of Minoan

*O*rnament has always held an important place in the Greek village, here on the island of Ithaca (top) *and on Koroni* (above). *A common feature of even the simplest one is the use of pebbles to create geometric patterns, as in the square of Nikia on Nissyros* (opposite).

culture. Their massive structures, fortifications and tombs for the most part, are often refered to as 'Cyclopian', possibly because later generations of peasants took them to be the work of giants and the one-eyed Cyclops (from Homer's *Odyssey*) was the paradigm of Greek gianthood.

The Trojan war, in which an Achean federation besieged that city, took place *c.* 1250 B.C. Odysseus' (Ulysses) wanderings ensued.

Around 1100 B.C. the Dorian Greeks arrived. The Acheans were vanquished, held out in the hills or escaped: notably as Aeolians taking up residence on the coast of Asia Minor (modern Turkey), and as Ionians on its offshore islands, particularly Lesbos, Samos and Chios.

The Archaic Age began around 800 B.C. It was during this that the qualities for which we most revere the ancient Greeks became evident. Homer flourished around 750 to 700 B.C.; the first Olympic Games were held in 776 B.C. Life-sized statues, often if the truth be known rather garishly painted, begin to appear in the 6th century. From 594 B.C. Solon started a series of reforms in Athens that we now regard as the dawn of democracy.

The Classical Age, high-water mark of the city state, is regarded as beginning around 500 B.C. The doughty (allied Greek) democrats beat off repeated assaults by the Oriental (Persian) despots at Marathon and elsewhere, often by the narrowest of margins and only when the Greeks could be dissuaded from bickering amongst themselves. Great and famous names, Pericles, Demosthenes, Praxiteles, Plato, flourished, often briefly (the really 'golden age' of Athens was only *c.* 461–429 B.C. and was pretty much riven by war), before the most famous name of all, Alexander, conquered all of Greece and much of the known world from 330 B.C. on, ushering in the Hellenic Age. But already three great European stereotypes were apparent: the democratic, individual and intellectual Athenians, the frippery disdaining and highly focused Spartans, and the essentially mercantile Corinthians.

From then on Greek history is very much subsumed in that of the eastern Mediterranean as a whole and its empires. The Roman one ensued, became Christian, was divided into two with, from A.D. 330, the eastern one based on Constantinople, also known as Byzantium. This empire extended for much of its life well beyond the boundaries of modern Greece, notably into the Balkans and Asia Minor, and survived for almost 1,000 years after the fall of Rome itself. Greek in one form was its *lingua franca* and in another the language of law, liturgy and scholarship. To this day 'the City' in Greek parlance refers to Constantinople, not Athens. Even more oddly to western ears it is not unusual for Greeks to still refer to themselves as 'Romans' (Patrick Leigh Fermor gives a memorable account of what he dubs 'the Helleno-Romanic dilemma' in his book *Roumeli*).

The village café, as seen here at Leonidio (opposite), is the traditional heart of (male) local life, though both it and its classic wood and rush chairs have become endangered species in metropolitan and tourist areas. The supermarket, however, still remains a more distant threat, and the general store is very much the norm at Dimitsana (above). This shop in Tinos (right), 'the Lourdes of the Aegean', caters for pilgrims to the nearby church of Panayia Evangelistria. Traditional utensils can still be found in older kitchens, although these examples (above right) are in Ipsounda's folk museum.

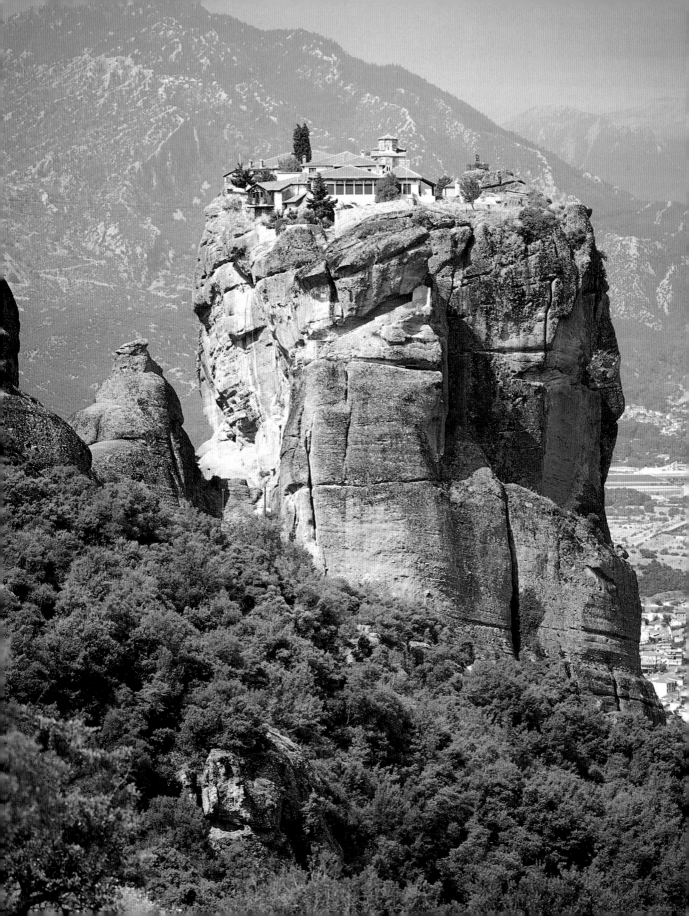

This hankering after a lost identity and lands (most of them still Turkish) is still a factor in Greek political life which sees betrayal to the west and menace to the east in roughly equal measure. The behaviour of the Franks during the twilight years of Byzantium, and most famously the diversion of a crusade to sack the softer and more lucrative target of Constantinople in 1204, was scarcely calculated to inspire confidence in their co-religionists (though the Orthodox and Catholic churches had finally split in 1054).

By the turn of the 15th century the Turks, having secured Asia Minor, began to absorb present-day Greece. Constantinople itself fell to them in 1453 and that was the end of Byzantium and New Rome. Various Frankish forces, notably the Venetian and Genoese, maintained a presence in Greece during the ensuing centuries of Turkish occupation, mostly on the islands and by force of arms (the Turks were never notable sailors), but also in enclaves on the mainland, and occasionally by treaty. The Greeks usually traded directly with the Franks or overseas rather than through any metropolitan centre.

It was the Greek Orthodox church, the remnants of the theocracy of Byzantium, that kept such learning and sense of nationhood as there was alive during these years. The Russian church, also Orthodox, was perceived as fraternal and certainly more supportive than the western one. Strong trading links with Russia resulted. As one of the more mercantile and seagoing peoples of the Ottoman Empire, strategically placed between east and west, the Greeks did well as shipowners and traders.

The War of Independence began in 1821, was espoused by western liberal opinion (Byron, Mark Twain and Herman Melville included) and independence was internationally recognized in 1830. A royal family was thoughtfully provided by the 'great powers'. The infant nation, however, was a small one. Modern Greece was assembled slowly and often painfully, with an ill-advised attempt (simply referred to as 'The Catastrophe') to regain lost lands in Asia Minor, ending in humiliation and defeat in 1922 and an exchange of Greek and Turkish populations. The Dodecanese had been passed in the post-war carve-up not to Greece but to Italy.

German and Italian occupation in 1941 elided into a bitter civil war between Communists and Royalists which ended with Communist defeat in 1949. The Truman Doctrine, wherein the United States pledged to fight Communism wherever it threatened democracy, and which led down the road to Korea and Vietnam, was first propounded in relation to the Greek civil war. Unfortunately, and not for the last time, the 'democrats' proved less democratic than the West might have wished. A military dictatorship from 1967 to 1974 was hopefully the last

*M*onasteries are rarely to be found in villages. Orthodox monks go to famous lengths to preserve their isolation. The monastery of Ayia Triada (opposite), one of many atop sheer rocks in the Meteora region, is a classic example. But even the smallest settlement in the Mani will have its own chapel (top). Dramatic settings, such as this on Santorini (above), are also common.

*W*hile hydrofoils now provide fast commuter-style services to islands such as Hydra *(opposite)*, villagers still tend to own and use traditional wooden craft, seen here on the Kefallonian coast *(top) and at Naoussa on Paros (above).*

gasp of undemocratic forces in the cradle of democracy, and the final instance of betrayal by the West, now that Greece is a full member of the European Union.

The European Union, along with tourism, however, is a greater force for change in the Greek village than any of the preceding: partly through a massive influx of wealth, partly through introducing a semblance of order where previously there was but a rather attractive and surprisingly effective form of anarchy. The often bare, austere, but immensely sociable *kafeneion*, where all (male) village life would from time to time convene, is being replaced by the telephone (if looking for the plumber, the priest, the bus driver or the captain of the ferry to buy an item in the nearest town), by the theme bar, and by television in the front parlour. Disputation, dialogue and a sense of community are the losers. So, paradoxically, can be the ease with which daily chores may be achieved.

Equally, the taverna, where it used to be as cheap to eat as it was to eat at home, not least because it was family owned and run, with no rent, national insurance, service, wages or taxes to inflate the bill, is now having to fall into line with the rest of Europe in these respects and be run as a 'proper business'. It is consequently in danger of becoming a venue only for special occasions and tourists. Fast-food outlets, on the other hand, are booming. The more we travel and the more we remove barriers, the more we make everywhere the same.

Not that the Greeks are any more ready than they have ever been to ditch the national identity to which they have demonstrated so fierce and tenacious a loyalty for so long. And in whatever way the bonds of the Greek village may be loosening, they are still a generation or two adrift from the Franks, still coherent communities able to fend for themselves in most things. Due to the poverty of the soil, few could be self-sufficient in food, but that and hospitals apart, the average Greek village could probably still survive without outside help. They still bake their own bread, sew their own wounds, make their own wine, build their own houses, if by the sea catch their own fish, mend their own machines, for the most part teach their own young, and provide their own transport to the nearest metropolis, while many households produce a measure of their own food. And if you visit one you are still likely to encounter most of its luminaries, from the priest to the dynamite fisher, in no time at all. The forum of Greek life is still in its public places.

The Mainland

*P*erhaps the most stirring landscape in all of Greece is that of the Mani at the south-western tip of the Peloponnese, with its villages of spiky tower houses huddled between the Taygetos mountains and the sea, seen here (previous pages) looking across to Exohori and the hinterland of Kardamili at the start of outer Mani. Village houses (above), here at Karitena, can often seem autochthonous – to have sprung from, or to be melting into the landscape.

*T*he Peloponnese is the most readily identifiable part of the Greek mainland, like a mis-shapen paw protruding to the south. The ancients named it thus (Pelops' island) after a quasi-mythical character who, like most of his ilk, came to a bad end (in this case being killed by his father and fed to the gods). Although joined to the rest of the mainland only by the 5-mile-wide isthmus of Corinth, it can never have been literally an island, for as is apparent from any photograph of the sheer-sided Corinth canal, the isthmus consists of solid rock which rises high above sea-level. There is, incidentally, a little-known and curious way of crossing the canal other than by the bridges from which the classic bird's-eye views are taken. At the canal's eastern end there is a sea-level bridge, which sinks beneath the canal's waters when a ship wishes to pass.

In medieval times western Europeans called the Peloponnese the Morea, a presumed reference to the mulberry, though opinions differ as to whether this was because it was supposed to be the shape of a mulberry leaf, or because the tree itself flourished here.

What the ancients had in mind in thinking of it as an island may well have been more than an (almost) literal truth. It is in many ways the historical heartland and redoubt of mainland Greece. If this was so, it was to prove a concept with a surprising and obviously unforeseen longevity. It was in the Peloponnese (at the monastery of Ayia Lavra, near Kalavrita) that the flag of modern Greece was first raised in revolt at the beginning of the War of Independence. It formed the bulk of the infant nation when its boundaries were first drawn, provided the provisional capital (Nafplion) until the mantle could be passed to Athens, and until very recently its eastern coastal communities were still effectively island ones. In the early nineteen-seventies some of these could still not be reached by road, you walked or went by boat. And where there were roads boat was still often the best way from Athens. Even today hydrofoils set the pace for public transport down much of this coast.

The Peloponnese

Arkadia

ARKADIA has been synonymous with bucolic bliss and Pan rampaging amongst the nymphs and shepherds beside leafy streams for hundreds of years. This arcadian vision is certainly one of our strongest preconceptions of Greece, owing much to seventeenth- and eighteenth-century paintings (such as those of Claude and Poussin). It is also the one most likely to leave the first-time visitor disappointed and wondering how on earth the heat and dust and raw mountains of Greece induced such cornucopian fantasies.

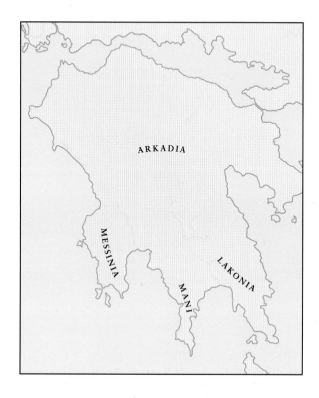

But though Greece today is undoubtedly seriously denuded (for which read goat-chewed) compared with ancient times, it is widely accepted that the climate of Arkadia has changed little since then and, in its mountain valleys in springtime at least, the idea of this as a peaceful, fertile and even mystical haven, albeit one with hard winters, snow and relatively high rainfall, does not seem so far-fetched. This is certainly how the ancients viewed this mountainous heartland of the Peloponnese, which wars and mainstream turmoil seemed to pass by, and where there dwelt a race of men and women who Pausanias tells us were regarded as autochthonous ('born of the soil'). There is historical evidence that some of the earliest inhabitants of Greece did indeed go to ground in these mountains when faced by later arrivals. Unlike the rest of the Greeks they never developed the city state (*polis*) whose inhabitants, perhaps hankering after a less complex existence as city-dwellers often do, seem to have romanticized the uncorrupted lifestyle of Arkadia they had left behind. After the arrival of the Turks in 1460 a final wave of Greeks took to the hills of Arkadia.

Leonidio

Street-life Leonidio style (above): *even the main street* (above right) *of this prosperous and relatively well-watered little community can be a joy to look at, while its walled gardens* (opposite) *are a rare luxury in lowland Greece.*

THIS SUBSTANTIAL LITTLE COMMUNITY will not dis-appoint those in search of arcadian echoes. It has had a strange recent history, having being briefly pro-pelled to provincial capital status in 1845 in the aftermath of independence (though its main build-ings date from before this episode) and then subsiding back into village life again this century. It is dramatically situated on the edge of a small half-moon plain which takes a bite out of the mountains of Arkadia here as they reach the sea. Its sturdy houses and fruitful gardens nestle beneath the sheer red cliffs of Mount Parnonas, which rises to 1,935 metres to form a near impenetrable barrier between inland Arkadia and this stretch of coast. It is a little less than three miles from the sea, the fairly uniform radius of the picturesque and fertile plain to which the town owes its modern prosperity (in the 19th century its wealth came from grazing cattle and sheep in the mountains in summer, and bringing them down to the valley only in winter).

By a happy touch of further symmetry, Leonidio is situated roughly at the centre of the plain's circum-ference, at a point where the cliffs form a bottle-neck in order for a high pass and a torrent through the mountains to debouch. Taking this, or at least the first stretch up through the mountains to Kosmas, where it appears to peter out in the sleepy and

beautiful main square (weave your way round the restaurant tables and the church and you will find it continues on the other side), is one of the most stir-ring drives in Greece. As it takes you up into what until recently was certainly wolf country, the road performs dizzying contortions as it doubles back upon itself and at one point, some 10 miles from Leonidio, the Monastery of Elona suddenly appears seemingly hanging like a white plaque slapped against the ravine high above the dramatic road.

Leonidio itself is a joy to wander through, both for its old cafés and houses, notably a twelfth-century fortified one which has been recently restored, and for some picturesque ruins, including some towers on the mountains, which have not. The river which irrigates the otherwise dry valley adds to the spectacle of the setting as well as making this a community of verdant, often walled, gardens: a rare luxury in Greece.

Most visitors, however, stay in nearby Plaka, the port of Leonidio served by hydrofoils from Piraeus. It is a compact and jolly spot, with a 'bijou' harbour with plenty of tavernas and good swimming from coarse sand and shingle. Apart from in August, this can be a peaceful spot to linger during the out-of-season months of the year.

Dimitsana

REPUTEDLY, this is ancient Teuthis (or Teftis), but this does not altogether accord with the location of that city as described by Pausanias when he deals with its involvement in the Trojan War. In any event Dimitsana today, dramatically situated at 2,789 feet (850 metres) between two hills overlooking the wild deep valley of the river Loussios, shows ample evidence of continuous occupation since the dawn of history. Some Cyclopean walls (those ascribed by even the ancient Greeks to a former race of giants, which is to say probably Mycenaean) survive in the Kastro on the western hill, as well as classical ones. Frankish and Norman influences are detectable in the ecclesiastic architecture of what is, for the most part, a medieval town (which once enjoyed a surprising share of the trade between western Europe and Asia Minor) of narrow cobbled streets and steps, picturesquely ramshackle houses, and superb views.

Doubtless because of its lofty remoteness, the village was well placed to play a hallowed role in the independence struggle. It became a centre of Greek learning (which in those days was becoming synonymous with resistance) after the foundation of its school in 1764. One of its more celebrated alumni was Archbishop Germanos of Patras, the man who was to raise the flag of revolt against the Turks at Ayia Lavra on 25 March 1821. During the ensuing war its fourteen powder factories made Dimitsana the arsenal of the revolution, while its branch of the Philiki Etaira (Friendly Society), the intellectual and political arm of the struggle, was also notably active.

One thing which differentiates Greek villages from their western European counterparts is the gap in the documentation of even, or in some cases especially, their relatively recent history. The fortunes of the mountain village of Dimitsana, however, have been well documented for the past 1,000 years; and the site has clearly been occupied since pre-history.

*D*espite its remoteness, the ramshackle medieval streets of Dimitsana
(opposite) and its ornate but often decayed balconies (above left)
are testimony to its past wealth, as are its numerous churches
(above, left and opposite below).

Ipsounda

Ipsounda (above and opposite), once one of the great metal-working centres of the Balkans, is another formerly prosperous but now somewhat depopulated village in a remote mountain setting.

STILL SOMETIMES KNOWN by its old name of Stemnitsa, or spelled Ipsounta, this is another dramatically sited (at 1,076 metres) and somewhat depopulated village, notable for its mellow medieval buildings and revolutionary associations. Built on the gentle wooded slopes of Mount Klinitsa (1,548 metres) it is trisected by deep gulleys into distinct quarters: the high, derelict Kastro, Ag Ioannis, to the east of the stream, and Ag Paraskevi to the west.

One thing these mountain villages of Arkadia have in common is that under 'Frankish' rule in the early Middle Ages their contact with the metropolitan centres of the rest of Greece declined and, faced by the impossibility of agricultural self-sufficiency, they tended to develop overseas markets instead.

Andritsaina, like Dimitsana, became a village of long-distance traders, while Ipsounda was for centuries one of the major metal-working centres of the Balkans. A notable folklore museum contains examples of this and other local crafts. Its scattering of chapels, including some Frankish ones incorporated into the Kastro, tend to be locked in order to protect their frescoes. Locals like to advance the claim that this was the first capital of Greece, since the first recorded convention of *klephtes* (the brigands mobilized as guerilla leaders by the Philiki Etaira) during the War of Independence took place here. The village square (*plateia*), with its shady trees, cafés and church, is a gem. Like most of these mountain villages today, it can be virtually deserted in winter.

*I*psounda's folklore museum contains examples of
traditional local arts and crafts such as these ikons
(opposite top). *The Trion Irerarhon church
(opposite below) is one of several medieval or
earlier ecclesiastical gems, some going back to the
10th century and incorporated into the remains of
the Kastro. The old streets (above) have typical*
mule-length steps (pack animals would find human-
stride ones hard if not impossible to negotiate). *As
they leave the village (overleaf right), mule tracks
would still be paved. These gates (top and above
right) offer glimpses into hidden worlds in the Kastro
quarter, where (overleaf left) many balconies still
incorporate examples of local metal-working skills.*

Karitena

KARITENA, also spelled Karitaina, believed to be a corruption of Gortys, the ancient site of which is nearby, has a somewhat dilapidated and abandoned air today. But once it was a thriving capital of some 20,000 souls, one of the more dazzling and, in a Greek context, incongruous Frankish strongholds of the Levant. They captured it in 1209 from the Byzantines, who had founded modern Karitena in the 7th century on the site of ancient Brenthe, whence the inhabitants of Gortys had decamped after its capture by the Slavs. Hugh de Bruyères built the castle, or *frourio*, a fine example of medieval fortification, from which to rule his extensive barony of 22 fiefs in 1254. His son Geoffrey was celebrated in the medieval ballad 'The Chronicle of Morea' as 'the Sire of Caritene', the very epitome of the chivalrous knight, his court renowned for its tournaments and the quests of courtly love. Karitena's beautiful setting in a natural defensive position above the Alpheios river (which Hercules famously diverted further down its course in order to cleanse the Augean stables) has provoked comparisons with that of Toledo.

With later additions, notably some Turkish towers, the *frourio* was still more than a match for the Turkish army of Ibrahim Pasha when Kolokotronis (one of the more celebrated freedom fighters) and his men holed up here in 1826 in an act of defiance credited with turning the struggle for independence. There is a fine view of the Alpheios gorge from its walls. There is also a remarkable semi-ruined medieval bridge across the river, with a chapel incorporated into a central pillar and one of its arches. This has featured (along with Kolokotronis) on Greek banknotes. What remains of Karitena's houses seems to reflect an embattled past, with small high windows, and often only cattle housed at ground-level (a useful source of extra heat in winter).

*N*ow with scarcely more than a hundred inhabitants, Karitena was once the seat of a major Frankish barony much given to displays of chivalry and presided over by the substantial thirteenth-century castle whose remains still dominate the site (opposite). *The little thirteenth-century chapel of Ag Nikolas (above) is the most notable of some forty churches and contains some well-preserved frescoes.*

Messinia

THE SOUTH-WEST OF THE PELOPONNESE has always been home to some of Greece's most prosperous farmers. Homer portrays Nestor as ruling in pastoral splendour from 'sandy Pylos' with all the virtues, and fruits, of good husbandry. The Spartans coveted Messinia, with wars between the two kingdoms and a semi-permanent state of helotry for the hapless Messinians being the norm for four centuries, until Epaminondas led them to victory in 371 B.C. Franks and particularly Venetians found this an advantageous area for trading bases, with its good harbours, plentiful produce and a strategic position on east-west shipping routes.

Peloponnesian ethnic jokes portray the Messinians as compulsive vendors; Kalamata (severely damaged in a recent earthquake) has a reputation for exporting pimps as well as for the plumpest (but not necessarily the most tasty) olives in Greece. Messinia remains relatively fruitful to this day, with probably the highest per capita rate of tractor ownership in Greece.

Modern Pylos, some miles from ancient Pylos, is also known as Navarino and it was in its bay that the naval battle of Navarino took place in 1827. The sinking of the Turkish fleet by a combined, but much smaller British, French and Russian one under the command of the British Admiral Codrington ended Turkish rule in the Peloponnese. The pleasant little town, as it has now become, was built with French help around a square commemorating the battle and has some wonderful old shops. Methoni and nearby Koroni were the 'eyes of the Peloponnese' for the Venetians, on either side of the most westerly of its three southern peninsulas. Their almost toy-like (though in Methoni's case scarcely small) forts remain their most striking features to this day.

Methoni was a major staging-post for medieval pilgrims on the way to the Holy Land. Its bay has silted up now, turning it into something of a beach resort, with the steady afternoon winds which swing around the fortress promontory on this tip of the Peloponnese a challenge to windsurfers as once they were to sailors.

Bijou medieval Koroni, with its leafy citadel, has an island feel, perhaps because its steep paved streets are better suited to mules than cars, perhaps because, superbly sited, it prefers to turn its back on the mainland and gaze across the Messinian gulf as islanders might to the distant Taygetos range which can be snow-capped into May. Turtles still nest on the nearby long sandy beach, one of the loveliest in Greece.

The Bourdzi tower (opposite), *originally Venetian but remodelled by the Turks in the 16th century, is linked to the massive citadel of Methoni* (overleaf right), *a major staging post between western Europe and the Levant throughout much of history.*

*T*he British Admiral Codrington is still *remembered in Pylos* (above) *where his naval victory clinched the independence of this gloriously endowed land* (below).

Koroni, the more gem-like twin of Methoni, was the Argive colony of Asine in ancient times and re-occupied by Franks in the early 13th century. It has a smaller but more intact Venetian citadel (opposite) above the town; its narrow cobbled streets and harbour (this page) give it an almost island feel. Note the classic wood and rush chair.

Details of Messinian secular life (this page) *contrast with the chapel of Ag Ioannis* (opposite), *one of several with a nunnery, creating a leafy oasis in Koroni's citadel.*

*T*he lion of St. Mark (right) *is a reminder of the Venetian origin of Methoni's fortifications which still guard the bay* (opposite). *The old sea-gate* (above) *was the point of entry for those landing at the Bourdzi tower* (p. 36).

Lakonia

LAKONIA, which occupies most of the south-eastern Peloponnese, and its capital Sparta have also entered our language. The militaristic Spartans had a reputation for being laconic: sparing of words, brief and concise in their speech. Nowadays we tend to apply 'laconic' to short, wry, witty responses, but neither humour nor indeed any frippery seem to have played much part in Spartan life which, like their unremarkable capital was, well, spartan. Pausanias when visiting these parts reports a case of someone being put to death 'for adding four new strings to the old seven-stringed guitar'.

If Lakonia and the images we have inherited of it was in many ways the antithesis of Arkadia from the start, this has not altogether changed. Lakonia today, at least in its most bleak and defiant region, the deep Mani, preserves its sense of austere, unyielding apartness.

The village of Kiparissi offers the most dramatic and beautiful demonstration of how cut off many of the communities on the eastern coast of the Peloponnese were from their neighbours until recently. It has but a narrow foothold between almost sheer mountains and the sea (for much of this coast there is not even that, the mountains plunging straight into the sea). And the only road down to it, built in the late nineteen-seventies, is one of the most breath-taking drives in Greece.

Shortly after the village of Harakas something amazing happens. You enter what looks like a short, narrow, very high gorge, only to discover when the right hand side of it drops away to reveal the sea below that however high the cliff above you to the left, there is suddenly about twice as much of it again below you to the right. The ensuing descent into Kiparissi hits every superlative, with wonderful views to islands offshore, a fort above, chapels built into the rock, a road that shaves the vast red cliffs so tightly that needles of rock are left between you and the abyss, and then greenery, some magnificent trees and then Vrissi, the first and most beautiful of the three villages which are often collectively referred to as Kiparissi (the other two are Paralia and Metropolis).

Vrissi means 'spring'. You pass Kiparissi's water supply, piped from the spring at the foot of the cliffs on the left as you enter Vrissi. Above the spring are three chapels tucked into the cliff, at least one of which will doubtless be flying the Greek flag. The upper two date from many years back, but the lower one was built only recently by the parish priest as a place for meditation.

Paralia means 'shore'. There is a beach here with good bathing for confident swimmers, a few rooms to rent, and the tiny harbour which so recently was the only way in and out of Kiparissi, save by foot or mule. It remains the preferred means of public transport access for passengers from Athens.

Kiparissi (opposite), three villages in one; until recently it was reachable only by sea, foot, or mule, but can now be approached down a breathtaking new mountain road.

*P*ara[*P*]aralia (opposite), *which means 'shore', has a tiny harbour looking across to Metropolis. Sea remains the preferred means of public-transport access for passengers from Athens. Shade (above left and right) is an essential feature of village houses: here in Vrissi donkeys still have their role; this one (left) is in nearby Gerakas.*

ONCE KNOWN AS MALMSEY and in former times the point of enshipment for the Malmsey wine much beloved of the British medieval aristocracy (so much so that the Duke of Clarence famously chose execution by drowning in a butt of it in Richard III's day), Monemvassia is one of the marvels of Greece. For once the hackneyed description (in this case 'the Gibraltar of the eastern Mediterranean') is entirely apposite. Always one of the last redoubts of the Peloponnese to fall to invaders, this great rock is sheer for much of its circumference. There is only one way in or up (thus its name, believed to be a corruption of the Greek for 'one entrance'): along a causeway from the mainland, along much of the rock's length and then finally through the pedestrian-sized gate in the first of a series of mainly Venetian fortifications which enfold the partially restored, primarily Byzantine town and the only feasible approach to the ruined fortress (as well as to the vestiges of its once larger upper town on the heights above).

Although much of the main street of the lower town has been colonized by shops and restaurants aimed at the tourist trade, walking just a couple of corners away from this artery can result in comprehensive but agreeable disorientation in alleyways so old and dark that one can wonder (for instance) whether one is contemplating an old but furred-up fountain, or a carving that is oozing water.

The restoration, so far as it goes (about half way), is recent and impeccable, if a touch sterile. What homes there are here are mostly holiday ones, whilst Gefyra, on the mainland end of the causeway, is where most people live. The climb from the lower town to the fortress atop the rock is not a taxing one save in the midday summer sun, and although there is little to see here in terms of buildings, apart from the utterly unforgettable church of Ayia Sophia on its clifftop perch, you will be rewarded by stirring views, birdsong and, unless the wind is up, utter peace.

Monemvassia

*M*onemvassia, a defensive site since Minoan times, was once a substantial settlement, with the main town occupying much of the skyline of the massive rock (below). *Now only ruins and a church remain at the summit. In later years the residents opted for a less obvious but still fortified presence on the lower slopes of the rock. The church of Ag Nikolas (opposite) has a sixteenth-century Venetian doorway.*

*E*ventually the lower settlement of Monemvassia, a
palimpsest of Byzantine buildings with Venetian
walls, itself fell into disrepair and is only now being
gradually restored.

The Mani

THE MANI IS WILD, splendid, unconquered country, the southern half of the mighty Taygetos range which in the north looms over Sparta and is one of the great physical divides of Greece. At Cape Tenaro, also known as Cape Matapan, the Aegean meets the Ionian at the southernmost point of the Greek mainland which is also the second most southerly point of the European continent after Tarifa in Spain.

The people, and their villages, famously match the drama of this land. These are almost certainly the last of the Spartans; all-conquering Rome left only this, as the Confederation of Free Lakonia, in all of the Peloponnese to manage its own affairs. According to one theory the Maniots may also be distant cousins of Napoleon, for Bonaparte is the literal translation of a common Greek name (but not, alas for the theory, a Maniot one) and Maniots had emigrated to Corsica a century before his birth. Whatever their pedigree, the Maniots are a disputatious bunch, and while the original inhabitants may have been disinclined to budge (the Corsican *émigrés* were a rare exception) many a fierce fighter, bloody but unbowed, has swollen their numbers and aggravated their temper by taking refuge here throughout history.

Such was their reputation that the Turks gave up on Mani and settled for a face-saving appointment of a Maniot chief as 'Bey' instead. A nominal tribute may have been fixed, but by all accounts it was rarely received.

Mani is commonly divided into inner and outer Mani, the division roughly according to the current boundary between Lakonia and Messinia, which runs just to the north of Itilo. Outer Mani today is thus not in Lakonia but in Messinia. This has not always been so. And there is no reason not to treat both parts of Mani, which have more in common with each other than with anywhere else, as one.

Of the two main approaches to the deep Mani, that down the west coast of the peninsula from Messinia is the most satisfyingly orchestrated. The mountains here are tumbling, towering and stupendous, and the hairpin drive to Kardamili, negotiating the ravines of Mount Taygetos, past increasing numbers of perched mini-forts, is unforgettable. These are the first intimations of the most distinctive feature of the Maniot villages, for on so wild, dry, stark and often forlorn a landscape, with so little room for crops, where even olive trees come shrub-shaped and bonsaied, disagreements between such

*T*he severity of the Mani and its defensive housing is softened in the outer Mani village of Kardamili by greenery, although even this has an aggressive air.

ferocious citizens, their ranks periodically swelled by yet more refugees with no taste for surrender (such as Cretans under Ottoman rule), were inevitable.

Vendettas became endemic, between neighbours, between families (which is to say clans), between neighbourhoods and between villages, and occasionally with whoever was running the rest of Greece. Even with independence, for which they fought as fiercely as any, the Maniots proved hard to assimilate into national life, not least because they promptly assassinated the infant country's first president.

The most visible effect of all this feuding is the Maniot tower house, minimally doored, reluctantly windowed, built ever higher to maintain strategic advantage over one's neighbour (hurling missiles down on to and thus destroying his roof could be a highly satisfactory conclusion to any Socratic differences); these huddle together not for mutual protection, as in the French *bastide*, but in mutual disputation to form villages which from afar resemble mini-Manhattans or, more sadly and frequently nowadays, three-quarters ruined, war-torn cities.

The most potent, indeed sole, force for halting or reversing this decline nowadays is tourism. Tower houses are being restored both by tourist boards and private enterprise for people to stay in, though they are rather gloomy to most tastes;

after all the Maniots built them to keep out just about everything, including the sun.

Kardamili is the first coastal village one reaches on this approach to Mani. Homer tells us in the *Iliad* that 'Kardamyle' was one of 'seven well-peopled cities' of the region which Agamemnon offered Achilles in an unsuccessful attempt to coax him out of his sulk over female captives at Troy. The acropolis of the old town, a mile or so inland, where the Maniot guerrilla leaders Kolokotronis and Mavromichalis would relax over a game of chess, using their troops as pieces during the War of Independence, has yielded evidence confirming more or less continuous occupation since Mycenaean times. It was a substantial Roman settlement. Pausanias, who records that the Emperor Augustus decreed one of the periodic boundary shifts which in this instance restored this part of Mani to Lakonia, retells Homer's story of how the sea-nymphs (or Nereids) once came ashore here. A church (dedicated to the Falling Asleep of the Blessed Virgin) now occupies the site once sacred to them.

The semi-abandoned medieval tower houses below the acropolis, which are all that now remains of the old town, are clustered around the eighteenth-century church of Ag Spiridon (an unusually far-flung residence for the patron saint of Corfu).

These towers are being slowly restored to accommodate tourists, though not without controversy, for the people of Kardamili are a conservative and relatively affluent lot, as disputatious as good Maniots should be, and not inclined to pursue over-zealously the tourist drachma if it means spoiling the view. Less controversial plans envisage some restoration of the ancient mule tracks, still paved but prone to become overgrown with disuse, which lead from the old village up into the mountains, the dramatic Viros gorge and mountain communities such as Tseria, Exohoria and Saidona which are in some measure being revived by the eagerness of foreigners to acquire and restore their houses.

The 'new' village of Kardamili on the sea-shore dates mostly from the 19th century and, although indisputably Maniot (Patrick Leigh Fermor, the literary patron of Mani, saw fit to make his home close by), it has a mellow charm and beauty not normally associated with the region. The square-cut, two- or three-storey (not tower) houses in warm-hued stone have wrought-iron balconies and gardens of astonishing variety and fruitfulness: in one far from spacious yard you can expect to spot bougainvillaea (practically standard), jasmine, quince, pomegranate, rose, giant geranium, pear, grape-vine, lemon, loquat, olive, pine and eucalyptus all jockeying for position. And over it all Taygetos looms and lowers, its escarpment dotted with cypresses and vaguely fortified spots often aswirl in cloud.

With plenty of places to stay and some good restaurants and cafés (but a beach of toe-stubbing pebbles) Kardamili makes an agreeable touring base for Mani.

Itilo (sometimes spelt Oitilo or called Vitylo) is where, at the ravine of Milolangadho which bisects the village, inner Mani begins. The Turkish castle and frontier post of Kalefa, built at the seventeenth-century high-water mark of Turkish power in Greece, stands watchful guard above. Homer records that Itilo sent men and ships to Troy. In ancient times the sanctuary of Sarapis was roughly where the castle now stands; Pausanias describes a wooden idol of Apollo in the market-place there. Napoleon visited Itilo, putting ashore at nearby Limeni, on his way to Egypt. No record seems to exist as to whether he was aware of his own putative links with the region, or whether he used the visit to investigate the matter further (the Corsican Maniots had come from Itilo). In those days this was the capital of Mani and home to some of its more powerful and piratical clans, and he was certainly interested in exploiting anti-Turkish sentiment. Itilo today is in sad decline and relatively unsuccessful in competing for a restorative injection of tourism. Neo (new) Itilo is a small seaside resort of recent construction on the shore below.

Limeni, between Itilo and the modern capital of Areopolis, and in its time port to both, is one of the few safe natural harbours in the region, though with the advent of roads it has lost its importance. It was once, along with Areopolis, home to the powerful, wealthy, and indeed pre-eminent Mavromichalis clan, who would have owed much of their prosperity to piracy and slave trading through here. One of their tower houses, now restored and oddly bland looking, and a couple of pleasant seaside tavernas (with a tendency to overcook the fish but much favoured by American Greeks on their summer roots trip) are the chief attractions in the cove today.

Some things have not changed much in Greece since the days of Byzantium and the two main contenders in the political arena are still the Blues (New Democracy) on the right and the Greens (nothing to do with ecology, but Pasok, the socialists) on the left. The Maniots have always been Blue and Royalist. This has had tangible results. Blue graffiti are everywhere in Mani, Green ones almost non existent. But most of all there are the roads. Effective land communications with the rest of Greece dates back only to the military dictatorship of 1967-74. The Maniots understand autocrats (even when they do not like them) and the Colonels returned the compliment by giving Mani the public utilities and, above all, the roads it had always lacked.

If Areopolis has eclipsed Itilo as effective capital of Mani during the past century it is at least partly due to this. It is now the first major Maniot community reached by the traveller from Athens. But it remains a dusty village of towers, churches and narrow streets, albeit with shops, tavernas and traffic to provide animation.

Ares, of course, was the god of war. But Areopolis is not so called after the ferocity of its inhabitants. At least not exactly. Tsimova, as it once was, was renamed in honour of the glorious role of the Mavromichalis clan and their followers in the War of Independence.

South of Areopolis, Mani is reduced to basics: tower houses, some approximating more to small castles and most in sundry states of collapse, come thick and fast now; there are occasional and often very beautiful chapels, while cacti seemingly predominate in a blasted landscape which is more fertile than it looks (hence the funds which built the chapels). This is often referred to as 'the shadow coast' and it can seem remarkably appropriate to this bright but sombre, silent landscape, seemingly half-abandoned but scattered with nests of towers casting long shadows, fleetingly swept themselves by the shade of clouds before they melt into the dark ravines and distant peaks of the mountain backdrop.

Kita (also known as Koita or Kitta) was always one of the more ferociously contested and powerful villages of Mani. Colonel William Leake, a British officer seconded to the Turks to advise them on their defences (should Napoleon choose to test them) at the beginning of the 19th century, reported the presence of almost 100 families and 22 towers. Kita was the site of the last recorded full-scale internecine battle in Mani, when the Kaouriani and the Kourikiani families set to in 1870. All the other residents of Kita fled or stayed indoors. A relief force of police arrived but was sent packing. Finally, the Prime Minister (himself a Maniot) sent in the army, but it took 400 troops with artillery to persuade the warring factions to mend their ways.

Perhaps the most striking of the restorations which are breathing life back into the tower houses and villages of Mani today is the EOT (national tourist office) one in the dramatically situated village of Vathia almost at the foot of Mani, which was reputedly founded by Cretans. Five houses have so far been restored (offering 12 rooms, some with dramatic sea views) in the village which still has a few permanent and nowadays peaceful inhabitants, for today's traveller has nothing to to fear from the Maniots. Colonel Leake, however, reported that he was counselled against passing through Vathia because of the ferocity of its feuds, one of which had been running for 40 years.

*E*choes of Rome: cypress trees bring a Latin touch to the tower houses clustered around the church of Ag Spiridon below the ancient acropolis of old Kardamili, the only place in Mani to have had a significant Roman past.

*I*tilo has the appropriate drama of setting to be the divide between inner and outer Mani (opposite), *heralding a starkly beautiful world. Napoleon, who possibly had Maniot blood himself, landed at Limeni* (below) *on his way to Egypt, hoping to stir up a Maniot revolt.*

*L*ife today in the Mani is much less tower-bound than in the past; this terrace (above left) *is in Tseria, near Kardamili, where many foreigners have made their homes. Kitta* (above), *always one of the more warlike villages, has not lost its ferocious mien. This corner of Platia* (left), *near Areopolis, has an almost monastic air which belies a warlike past. From the otherwise stark and unremarkable little harbour of Yerolimenas* (opposite) *there is a dramatic view of the ancient nautical crossroads that is the southern tip of the Peloponnese.*

Ο ΜΑΣΤΡΟΛΙΑΣ
ΟΥΡ Η ΜΗΤΣΑΚΟΥ

*D*etail from a fresco in the Mavromichalis family church of Ag
Ioannis in Areopolis (opposite); *the capital is named after the
ancient god of war, but this little shoe shop* (above) *no longer serves
fighting men.*

*S*ome of the finest examples of Maniot fortified tower houses are those in Vathia (these pages) which, as in many villages, have been restored under a government scheme to provide accommodation for tourists. From the far distance such villages can seem like mini-Manhattans; closer, a more intimate scale is revealed.

Overleaf
*C*hristianity came late to Mani, probably not much before the 10th century, which marked the start of a flurry of religious construction. This palimpsest of religious iconography (left) is in the now roofless tenth-century church of Ag Pendelimon in Ano Boularii. The eleventh-century Byzantine church of Taxiarchis in Harouda (right) has some notable and well-preserved frescoes.

Pelion, Epiros, Evritania

Pelion

PELION is one of the most lyrical regions of Greece, fruitful, leafy and alive with the sound of running water. The name is commonly used to refer to the peninsula formed by the southern slopes of Mount Pelion (which rises to 1,551 metres, 5,089 feet), though it is more correctly Magnesia. Pelion has long been celebrated for its villages, and in Ottoman times was confusingly (given the presence on the other side of Greece of the Zagorochoria) referred to as the villages of Zagora, after the most eminent of their number. Early nineteenth-century travellers reported that this was the richest and most cultured region of mainland Greece, with the finest houses.

Mount Pelion itself was famously piled upon Mount Ossa in Greek mythology as a stepping stone to heaven by the giants during their tussle with the gods. And the strange thing is that long ago, too long one imagines to be part of any human memory, something of the sort seems to have happened: Thessaly was once an enormous lake until a convulsion between Mounts Pelion and Ossa opened up the Vale of Tempe between them and the waters gushed out into the sea.

Magnesia, lush, mountainous, and heavily forested, was ever the stuff of myths and a certain trepidation, the home of wild, hairy, Stone Age men (lapiths), of strange but wise and ancient creatures (centaurs), not to mention nymphs (such as Cyrene) given to wrestling with lions. Most classical references to Magnesia are so ancient as to be quasi-mythological. Cheiron the centaur, half-man, half-horse, was said to have been the tutor of both Achilles and the doctor-god Asklepios. His name gave us 'surgery' (via 'chirurgery'). The people of these hills and forests, an ancient race, may have been credited with shamanistic powers by later arrivals. Iolkos, close to the city of present day Volos, was the port from which Jason sailed in quest of the Golden Fleece.

*M*akrinitsa (opposite) *was founded in the 13th century by refugees from Constantinople; a classic shady and well-watered Pelion village, it is well endowed with churches, restored old houses with tourist accommodation, and splendid views.*

History and archaeology are less informative about the settlement of Pelion. Its forests have kept their secrets well. Modern village life was a direct consequence of the monasteries which by the 12th century were sufficiently numerous to invite comparisons with Mount Athos. These seem to have formed the nucleus of small settlements which in turn acted as a magnet to new arrivals, especially after the Turkish occupation of Thessaly in the 15th century had prompted the usual exodus to the hills (it is no coincidence that so few of the more ancient villages of Greece are lowland ones). Makrinitsa and Portaria began this way. So did Ayios Lavrentios (which kept the name of the founding monastery), while the monastery of Metamorphosis begat Zagora.

Pelion prospered under the Turks, who as usual occupied the lowlands and, as was also often the case, not only left the highlanders alone but granted them privileges and exemptions.

Silk, or more precisely the mulberry trees which grew in the sunny but cool and well-watered glades amongst the oak,

chestnuts, plane and walnuts of Pelion, was the reason for the Turks gazing kindly upon the villages whose silk was exported to much of Europe and the Orient. Zagora, Portaria and Milies were the most successful silk villages. Tanning, felt-making and copper-work also contributed to the fame and prosperity of Pelion which was always solidly underpinned by a thriving agricultural sector.

As was also often the case, the villages traded direct with the outside world rather than through any metropolitan centre. They built their own ships at Trikeri, at the tip of the peninsula, and traded via the Venetians. The region's prosperity peaked in the mid 18th century and then collapsed dramatically with independence. The wars and revolutions which led up to the 1881 union with Greece disrupted trade, and exhausted the people and much of their wealth. After the departure of the Turks and a devastating earthquake in 1885 the nearby port city of Volos took most of Pelion's trade and population. There was no longer any need to live in the mountains.

The villages reward study today not only for their beauty, but because there is nothing else quite like them in Greece. No other mountainous region has such a density of villages with no obvious capital. The Pelion house also epitomizes the Greek village house in all its stages of development, culminating in an elegance that no others attained. The lower floors are stone. They started, as almost every house in rural Greece started, as *kalivia*, pens, sheds, stables. This became the *katoyi* (downstairs) with the addition of another stone floor or two with small, usually barred windows, for storage, and a measure of human habitation.

They could have continued in this style, defensively upward (as in Mani) and/or outward (as in the Zagorochoria). Or they could just have stopped, as in much of the rest of Greece, and capped the production with the schist tiles which are characteristic of this region and of much of mountain Greece. Here they seem to work the schist more than in the Zagorochoria; one is more likely to encounter tile-knappers at work, and the houses themselves generally have thinner, less ponderous tiles.

Certainly the need for defence was always a consideration. Traces of a *zematistra* through which boiling oil could be poured on unwelcome visitors can be seen above many a Pelion front door. This was later modified to projecting bars on an upstairs window, the better to see who was below before deciding how best to greet them.

*R*oadside shrines, like this one near Portaria, are to be found throughout Greece (above), well cared for and housing an icon, a lamp or candle and a bottle of olive oil. The sound and sight of water, often so abundant that it is just left to cascade upon the road (left), is a striking feature of Pelion, compared to the aridity of much of the rest of Greece.

But in Pelion something quite different happened. With increased prosperity and self-confidence, the houses blossomed out. For their owners created not simply the standard small dark winter rooms (*himerino*), in which one could huddle round a fire, or even just the somewhat rarer larger and lighter summer room (*kalokairino*) as well, they added a storey to the traditional inward-looking stone house; they made it of wood, and they made it bigger than the floors below, so it projected out from the house all around (*saknisi*). They could do this because the houses in Pelion had been built well apart to allow water a free run past them down the steep terrain in heavy rain.

And thus high above the ground and safe from intruders, they indulged in the ultimate luxury of something rather like modern urban loft living, with big unbarred bay windows in which one might loll about on cushions at the end of spacious rooms with fine ornaments and decorations, carvings, stained glass, and even frescoes. Elements of western living, armchairs and bookcases, also arrived here early. In no other villages of mainland Greece was the living so gracious or so outward-looking in the 19th century. A further element of exoticism was added by Greeks of the diaspora, notably ones who had made good in Egypt, making their homes here and importing elements of Moorish architecture, notably façades with high arches on thin pillars.

The villages of Pelion never suffered the worst effects of depopulation. They may be mostly secondary homes today, but many of these belong to the inhabitants of nearby Volos who love to escape to the cool of Pelion on a summer's night.

Portaria (650 metres, 2,133 feet) is the prime example of such seductiveness, less than 10 miles from the city, with good views down to Volos and the Pegasitic Gulf, the sea on the inland side of the Pelion peninsula. It no longer has the exceptional *archontikaspitia* described by Dodwell, an English traveller in the early 19th century, but has no shortage of the instant charm which draws locals and tourists alike into these mountains, with all the Pelion trademarks of a beautiful, spacious square (*plateia*), where one may sit in cafés under plane trees, enjoying the sound of running water.

It is at Makrinitsa (700 metres, 2,297 feet) that one may appreciate the Pelion *plateia* at its most dramatic. For here, the steepness of the terrain is such that what has become the principal *plateia*, that by the beautiful little church of Ag Ioannis, had to be built both by cutting into the mountain and by building out from it, making it at once both an amphitheatre and a balcony, not to mention a memorable belvedere. Ag Ioannis and the former monastery of the Panayia, on the older upper level of the square, were centres of Greek learning and hence resistance during the Turkish occupation. A nearby street is named after Charles Ogle, killed here by the Turks, it is said in cold blood, in 1878, while reporting on the independence struggle for the London *Times*.

Makrinitsa, one of the more tightly built villages of Pelion, is well endowed with churches, restored houses with accommodation for tourists, and the works of a grand eccentric peripatetic painter, Theophilos. He was a late nineteenth-century primitive given to dressing up as Alexander the Great who asked no more of life, and his hosts, than board, lodging, painting materials and a surface (preferably a wall) on which to paint. The Café-Ouzeri Theophilos behind Ag Ioannis has one of his frescoes; influences going back to classical times are clearly discernible in his work which is also full of life, naive yet impressionistic. Others are to be found scattered around the villages, though the Kontos house at Anakassia, on the way up from Volos, now a small Theophilos museum, is the best place to see these. He was not the only painter who flourished in the Pelion villages in their prime. Drakia was a veritable den of painters at one time and was particularly well-endowed with frescoed *archontikaspitia* until it bore the brunt of the 1955 earthquake.

The church of Agia Marina in the leafy little village of Kissos is one of the finest in Pelion and contains examples of the work of one of the region's more prolific peasant painters, Paghonis.

Tsangarada (499 metres, 1,637 feet) is close to the relatively steep and rugged terrain of the west coast and one of its best beaches (Milopotamos). This is the largest Pelion village after Zagora, but it sprawls peacefully beneath the trees and is subdivided into four communities. That of Ag Paraskevi has in its *plateia* what is reputedly one of the oldest (local claims start at one thousand years) and certainly one of the biggest (15 metres, 49 feet in girth) plane trees in Greece, its great limbs propped up nowadays by concrete crutches. Tsangarada is notable for its flowers, gardens full of roses, snapdragons, hollyhocks, lilies and carnations, and for its water. The days when Greeks would fiercely dispute the merits of this spring or that may have given way to indifferent tap water and bottled drinking water from the supermarket. But not in Tsangarada. Try some from one of its fountains.

Milies takes us back towards the Pegasitic Gulf coast with its gentler terrain and more protected shores. This has long been the cultural centre of the peninsula. The cave where Cheiron was supposed to have taught is here. The library and school of Milies was one of the most important in Greece towards the end of Ottoman rule. And as was often the way, it thus became home to one of the early 'friendly societies' which plotted revolt. It was in Milies that Anthimos Gazi raised the Thessalian standard of revolt in 1821. Nearby Vizitsa, more beautiful but less animated, is a showcase for *archontikaspitia*, and has some of the finest for tourist occupation in Pelion.

Stone beyond stone, yet the result is neither cold nor stark; Pelion villages, such as Makrinitsa (above and opposite), feel warm and alive; roofs look like the scales of some slumbering creature. Many of the grand old mansions (archontikaspitia) have been restored (above right) to past splendours. This kiosk in Kissos (right) has been painted with trailing plants, doubtless inspired by the local foliage, while a nearby public fountain babbles in distinctly Pelion style.

The neatly tiled tower of Ag Dimitrios overlooks the Pagasitic Gulf near Vizitsa, the village with some of the finest restored houses with tourist accommodation in the region.

The church of Ag Marina in Kissos (left), one of the finest in Pelion, is dedicated to a female saint who disguised herself as a boy to become a monk. Planes are the traditional Greek (and indeed Levantine) tree of shade, and this (below) in Tsangarada claims to be the biggest and one of the oldest in Greece.

Running water (left) is never far away from a shady Pelion plateia (square). Just off Plateia Theophilos in Makrinitsa (opposite) is a café containing frescoes by the peripatetic painter and grand eccentric of that name.

A fresco in the narthex of Ag Taxiarchis church in Milies (opposite);
*the village has a long tradition of learning stretching back to the
semi-mythological times of Cheiron the centaur. The ubiquitous free-
standing concrete stairway of Greece is here (above left) softened by
flowers in Makriarki. The fruits of Pelion can also be tasted as preserves
(left). A little chapel of the Virgin adjoins Ag Nikolas in the leafy
cool of Portaria (above).*

*T*he height of bliss for Greeks on a summer's day: shade, running water, flowers and good company, as in Makrinitsa (above left), *Milies* (top right), *the* plateia *of Tsangarada* (above) *and Portaria* (left and opposite). *Most of Greek social life takes place in the street and public places and in Pelion the* plateia *has evolved into a vibrant space.*

Epiros

THE NORTH-WESTERN part of Greece, like Macedonia, was always regarded as somehow 'other', neither exactly foreign, nor exactly Greek, by the ancients, yet both today excite feelings of nationalistic fervour in hotter Greek breasts. The Epiros (the 'mainland' or 'continent', as it certainly is when viewed from the Ionian Islands) once extended into present-day Albania. It contains some venerable ancient sites: that of the oracle at Dodona, second only to that of Delphi, and the Necromanteion (near modern Parga), the gateway to Hades, where Odysseus (Ulysses) consulted the oracle of the dead. In the first years of the 19th century the Epiros found fame as the fiefdom of Ali Pasha, Byron's tales of whom launched the vogue for barbarian chic.

The Epirots are famed as mountain men and shepherds. As nomads they scorned village life. As semi-nomads, which some still are, they would only consent to being housed in winter. The Epiros' finest and oldest villages therefore are mountain ones, and pre-eminent amongst these are the Zagorochoria.

The Zagori Villages

Of the 46 once prosperous villages of the Zagori (collectively known as the Zagorochoria), only the western ones escaped major damage in the wars of this century: firstly by the Turks in the Balkan War of 1912-13 which resulted in Epiros becoming part of Greece, then again by Germans avenging partisan activity in World War II, and finally during the Communists' last stand at the end of the bitter civil war which followed liberation.

The Zagori is a high limestone region of wild and magnificent grandeur in the north Pindos range of the Epiros, its more remote areas still the haunt of nomadic shepherds, wolves and bears. As befits its inaccessibility (roads are relatively recent arrivals) this was yet another area to which, faced by the hopelessness of policing it, the Turks pragmatically granted special privileges the better to concentrate on milking more fertile and tractable lowland communities.

The Zagori village of Aristi (opposite), though strikingly situated before Mount Astraka, is still wealthy and workaday enough to have survived without expensive restoration. Wolves and bears still live in these mountains.

The most striking of the western Zagorochoria, which are in largely self-created pockets of considerable fruitfulness in an otherwise hostile terrain, are those perched by the Vikos Gorge, possibly the most dramatic mountainscape in all of Greece. Here the Voidhamatis ('ox eye') river passes through cliffs which tower, almost sheer in places, for up to 1,000 metres on either side.

Wander down to one of the most vertiginous and accessible viewing spots for the gorge, that from the tiny monastic eyrie of Ayia Paraskevi below the village of Monodendri, and it is easy to see how it is that these villages blend so perfectly with the landscape. For all around lie what seem to be perfectly prepared building materials simply waiting to be used: the local limestone in schistic form naturally sliced and sundered into tile and even brick shapes and sizes. Indeed, above Monodendri, on the road to another even more dramatic and less visited lookout point, that of Oxias, some of the rockscapes, naturally cleft here both vertically as well as horizontally, can easily be mistaken at first glance for man-made structures, such as Cyclopean walls or Oriental temples.

If there are certain similarities between the villages of the Zagorochoria and those of Pelion on the opposite side of the mainland this is not altogether coincidental. Travelling bands of builders (*bouloukia*) were responsible for much of the professional building in Greece up until this century, and it was *bouloukia* from the mountains above Ioannina who built the *archondika* houses of Pelion.

The most obvious difference between the Zagorochoria and the villages of Pelion is that the former are more defensive, fortified against both greater cold and greater danger of attack from animals and men than ever existed in Pelion. In Zagori each house has its own defences: usually a high wall (the *oviros*) enclosing a courtyard and those walls of the house with otherwise accessible windows or doors. This outer wall is itself entered only through a pair of magnificently barbaric heavy wooden doors, studded for greater strength with horse nails and other ironwork (on some of the older houses the wood seems to be gracefully melting away, leaving just the ironwork).

This doorway is roofed and tiled with the slabs of rock which are so characteristic of the houses themselves, and opens into a world more private and secure than that of any Cycladic courtyard. It is also liable to be both surprisingly and lyrically

*G*reek spirit: Ioannis Harisis (aged 93) of Vitsa, one of the old but unbowed mountain men of Zagori, lived through the many wars which almost destroyed the eastern Zagori villages. Megalo Papingo (opposite) one of the most beautiful of the western villages, yields glimpses into the calm of its secret gardens.

beautiful, for these houses, *archondika* almost all, are an unusual blend of ostentation with defensiveness. Fruit trees, flowers and cats slumber within these private gardens. The unnatural prosperity of the Zagorochoria came to an abrupt end after 1868 when the Turks withdrew their privileges. Widespread decline. emigration and dilapidation resulted. Only in the last twenty years, with the advent of roads, tourism and European Union subsidies, has this process been halted and in most instances reversed.

The most obvious barometer of a village's fortunes today are the roofs of its houses; the prosperous ones with touristic potential have the traditional roofs of more or less naturally formed but hand-finished stone tiles (*schistoplakes*). When viewed from above (as classically they may be from the upper village of Vitsa) these seem to form a living rock which curves and flows, as if it were the scales of some great sleeping reptile. Other villages (such as Aristi), which managed to struggle along reasonably well before the advent of tourism and conservation orders, will have plenty of red-tiled roofs, whilst those which hit the bottom and have yet to recover have a high proportion of corrugated iron roofs, or no roofs at all. Even the most prosperous villages still have only pockets of houses fully restored to their original state.

Monodendri and Vitsa are within sight of one another (a common defensive strategy which enabled villages to warn their neighbours of approaching danger) above the upper reaches of the Vikos Gorge. Both have upper and lower villages. In Monodendri (the more touristic of the two) the upper village is where most visitors stay and villagers live, but its *plateia* is little more than a curve in the road. The lower village is both more picturesque, quieter and much better situated, almost on the gorge.

Vitsa is less huddled together and is to many tastes the more attractive of the two, its upper quarter having the views and the lower quarter being the more pleasant to sit or wander in. Walking down the cobbled mule paths of the Zagorochoria, ingenious multi-purpose constructions designed for pedestrians, animals, wheeled vehicles and water catchment alike, is to appreciate the magnificent combination of strength and beauty of these houses. Flowers and fruit trees provide splashes of colour as they peep over walls, vines often provide shade overhead, classic circular columns support balconies of wood and wrought iron, the beetle-browed stone roofs have their eaves sometimes only a metre above the ground, whilst either above all this or rolling away into the distance are the mountains.

Papingo and Mikro Papingo, a couple of miles apart at the other end of the gorge, offer a completely different perspective on it. Here the bluffs at the end of its most dramatic section (it continues in relatively pedestrian style for a few more miles downstream) tower up to 1,000 metres above the villages, inviting comparison with Yosemite in California or Lauterbrunnen in Switzerland viewed from their valley floors.

Of the two, the less visited Mikro Papingo is arguably the most attractive and certainly the most dramatically sited, being the closest to the feet of the Pyrgi ('towers') as the bluffs are called.

Papingo itself still has a fairly healthy non-touristic economy; cows, pack-horses and bell-wearing dogs are frequently to be encountered in the lanes, whilst in the mountains above the now only semi-nomadic but still laconic Sarakatsans (who regard the villagers as hopelessly effete) may still be encountered with their flocks and dogs.

The classic Vikos Gorge walk, that from Monodendri to Papingo, is signposted as six hours, but even the young and fit often find it takes them more like nine. Walkers can expect to cross some splendid examples of the stone pack-horse bridges (also sometimes called 'Turkish bridges', though not by the Greeks) for which the region is famed. Motorists may spot these near the village of Kipi. The village of Vikos itself, easily reached and close to Papingo, is strangely overlooked by most commentators yet offers the best view along this unforgettable chasm.

Previous pages

*T*erracing maximizes space and provides a firm hold for crops and houses on the hillside at Mikro Papingo (left). As you enter the village the tree-shaded square by the church with its mini campanile is a good place to sit and offers splendid views.

*O*ld tracks such as this one (above) in Vitsa are more complex than they look, coping with the mule stride, the shorter human step and channelling-off rainwater. The reason the houses blend so well with the landscape is that much of the building materials, particularly these schistic roofing slabs (above right) in Vitsa, are literally lying around the mountain sides waiting to be used. This house in Vitsa (right) is also a small pension.

*T*he once nomadic shepherds of the Vitsa region (above) *still tend their flocks, and savour ewe's milk, in a way their ancestors would recognize. Even the sheepdogs have bells. Vines in Mikro Papingo (left): although Zagorachoria villagers have made their own wine for centuries, the nearest commercial wineries are those of Zitsa whose slightly sparkling whites and rosés can be savoured in Zagorachoria tavernas.*

*T*o sort the sheep from the goats, look at their tails: sheep have hanging ones but those of goats stick up. These goats (above) are grazing where the Vikos gorge (opposite) opens out near the Papingos. Nearly 1,000-metres-high in places, this limestone canyon, created by the Voidhamatis ('ox eye') river, is a place of sublime and savage grandeur.

*K*lavsi (opposite) *is dominated by its substantial church* (above); *the village lies snugly in wooded hills, typical of Evritania, above the Karpenesiotes valley, south of Karpenissi.*

Evritania

THE WOODED MOUNTAINS of Evritania, around Karpenissi, are still quite impenetrable in places. This region, however, is now becoming a favoured summer holiday area for Athenians and is sometimes promoted as 'the Switzerland of Greece'.
It is often referred to as *agrafa*, 'unwritten', because successive rulers (notably the Turks) have failed to make much headway into the region. Many of the present inhabitants are returnee Greek-Americans. Most of the villages, such as Klavsi, have economics based on forestry. This area does, however, include some of the finest undisturbed villages of the Greek mainland and amply repays the effort of getting there. Mountain, forest and terracotta roofs combine in an extraordinary and forceful rural symphony.

The tiled and curved dome of Megalo Horio's church (opposite) is in complete contrast to the rectilinear houses behind: sub-Alpine style with verandahs to catch the sun, as in Koryschades (left and far left), one of the region's most attractive and substantial villages. Donkeys, as here in Megalo Horio (below), remain a practical means of transport in so unyielding and mountainous a terrain.

*M*ountain flowers and herbs give the best honey: these hives (right) are at Megalo Horio (above), also seen (opposite) from Mikro Horio, with the peak of the Kaliakouda mountain behind.

The Islands

The blue and white of the Greek islands: to sail into the sea-filled caldera of Santorini's still hissing volcano (preceding pages) is to experience one of the great arrivals of the world, while Mykonos (above) fulfills all our expectations about the architecture of the Greek islands.

For us, though not necessarily for the Greeks themselves, Greece without islands is unimaginable. It is to a significant degree an island nation, with over 160 permanently inhabited islands and as many as 1,400 more if one accepts less stringent definitions. They are not in the least peripheral to the nation's life. Board a metro train in central Athens, exit about 20 minutes later at Piraeus, cross the road, and you are in the islands' transport system.

The island capitals for the most part do not slot easily into familiar categories. For a start, many of the smaller ones are divided into skala *(harbour) and* hora *(town or village). In the larger islands (Rhodes, Crete, Corfu) there is no such distinction, the capitals have long been substantial, powerful, to some degree fortified, and unarguably towns.*

The skala *would have scarcely been inhabited at all until the 19th century. Instead, everybody lived in the more defensible* hora *atop a nearby hill. Just how nearby (and whether they have subsequently merged into one) would be a matter of local geography. But preferred areas of settlement from the dawn of history would combine a sheltered harbour with a nearby hill.*

In some respects these communities now have the appurtenances of towns: not only harbours but airports, civil servants, substantial churches and hotels. But that is more an accident of location than a reflection of their way of life: a similar number of dwellings on the mainland would never be so endowed. In that sense they are only villages, though it is more appealing to think of them as the last vestiges of that Platonic ideal, the polis, *just big enough to have the necessities of life, but still small enough for all its inhabitants to be known to one another and to have a sense of community.*

The Cyclades

THE CYCLADIC VILLAGE, for us, is the very symbol of Greece: a huddle of blazing white houses set in an eye-flinching rockscape between the great blues of the sea and the sky. But symbols after all are a form of shorthand, and the beauty and uniqueness of the Cycladic villages are not the eternal verities we might imagine. They have not, for instance, even been white for long. On the contrary, concealment was for centuries the uppermost decorative concern of the Cycladic householder in these pirate-infested waters, and he achieved this by the simple means of an unplastered, unpainted exterior. Exactly when whitewashing became the norm is unknown, but it was probably only within the last two centuries, and as much for hygienic and nationalistic purposes (the white antiseptic lime wash combining satisfyingly with the blue-painted woodwork to form the national colours) as for any aesthetic consideration.

It is possible to argue both for and against the Cyclades as the epitome of Greekness. On the one hand they have managed, largely due to their status as isolated and relatively barren rocks, to be bypassed by most of the major events of Greek history since Hellenistic times (notably an oppressive Turkish occupation). Nor did they nurture any great centres of post-classical Greek learning during that time which matched the fame of those of more prosperous and strategic islands such as Chios and Patmos, though both Andros and Paros had schools of note.

But on the other hand, it could be argued, the Cyclades had once been pace-setters of Greek culture, notably in the plastic arts. Some statuettes from the now uninhabited island of Keros dating from around 2500 B.C. in the Athens Archaeological Museum are the earliest known three-dimensional European works of art. So perhaps the fact that the Cyclades were left pretty much to their own devices for so long during the subsequent dark ages of Greece enabled a more genuine (and in some opinions purer) vernacular culture to survive and grow here than in the rest of Greece.

If so, this is nowhere more manifest than in the fabric of the villages themselves, which evolved unencumbered by formal architectural concepts or planning and yet have a manifest logic: the small windows and the maze of streets would have baffled raiders and winds alike, while the flat roofs and the piling of dwellings one on top of the other (or even arching them across the streets) maximized the use of space and

increased the defensive nature of the huddle, not least by affording increased mobility above ground-level to defenders.

The Cyclades (or Kyklades in Greek, which has no letter 'c') took their name in ancient times from the circle (*kyklos*) they were perceived as forming around the sacred island of Delos. Their constituency has varied over the years, but today their political grouping as a prefecture, with Ermoupolis in Syros as its capital, comprises some thirty islands.

Their history (unlike that of the Ionian) has been diverse. But most were part of the Frankish (and somewhat Ruritanian) Duchy of the Aegean which did not fall to Turkish rule until 1566, over a century after Constantinople. Tinos (which remained Venetian until 1715), Thira and Syros retained strong Frankish (which was also to say Roman Catholic) links and communities thereafter. But the rest of the islands, though nominally Turkish, had no such thing as a Turkish ruling class and were effectively self-governing, though subject to annual revenue-collecting visits by an admiral of the Turkish fleet. They were briefly annexed by Russia in the 1770s, a curious episode which was to end in the epoch-making, because highly profitable, dispensation from the Turks allowing certain Greek island ships to trade under the Russian flag. This was to be the basis of many early Greek shipping fortunes – and the foundation of the country's strong maritime tradition.

Syros

SYROS, the capital of the prefecture of the Cyclades, has always been relatively prosperous. Homer refers to it as being rich in flocks and grain. Its main town, Ermoupolis, is named after the Greek god of commerce. Strategically situated on the shortest sea route between western Europe and the Bosporus, while at the same time being the closest of the Cyclades to Piraeus, it has always been of more than passing interest to traders and navigators. French, Genoese and Venetian communities retained a presence here throughout much of the Turkish occupation. Its Catholic community enjoyed French protection during the War of Independence. Although it accepted refugees it was not otherwise involved.

Syros' finest hour came with independence (it was a serious contender for the new nation's first capital) and the eclipse of sail. Its position rocketed it into sudden prominence as the primary coal bunkering port of the eastern Mediterranean in the last century, and then into just as sudden a decline in this one as oil replaced coal.

The most obvious legacy of this brief flowering is a very fine French-inspired Neoclassical lower town. The main square, where doves skid across the shiny marble flagstones as they come into land and you can witness one of the finest evening *voltas* (the Greek equivalent of the Spanish *paseo*) in the islands, has even been compared (over-enthusiastically) with St. Mark's in Venice, whilst the architect of La Scala designed for the town a scaled-down version of his triumph in Milan.

But its longer history is reflected in the villages which occupy the twin peaks of the upper town. Ano Syros, which retains the fabric of a medieval Cycladic village, was built by the Catholics around their Cathedral of St. George, whilst their Orthodox neighbours built Vrondato around their church of Anastasi.

The capital of the Cyclades, Ermoupolis on Syros, has a more sophisticated architecture than the rest of the island group, including strong French influences in the lower town.

*M*any Cycladic capitals have no need of pedestrian precincts since the quickest way of getting about them is via stairways such as these in *Ano Syros* (this page).

*A*dmiral Miaoulis, whose statue
stands in front of the
town-hall (above), was the
outstanding naval officer of the
Greek revolution. In his pirate
days he was once captured and
briefly held by Nelson who, like
so many Britons, was readily
charmed by the picturesque
side of the Greek character.
The Orthodox church of Anastasi
(overleaf left) *tops Ermoupolis's
second peak, that of Vrontado
(left). Good Friday is a time for
processions and religious finery
in Ano Syros (overleaf right).*

Tinos

TINOS is an island of pilgrimages, dovecotes, some of the most skilled stonemasons in the islands, and a haunting fruitfulness. Don't be surprised if some of the ladies (for some reason it is always the ladies) don gloves and special knee-pads and crawl up the street from the boat on their hands and knees. This is 'the Lourdes of the Aegean', the spiritual heart of modern Greece (much as nearby Delos was of ancient Greece), and they are heading in penance or supplication up the hill to the church of Panayia Evangelistria. This is the home of a miracle-working icon of the Virgin attributed to St. Luke and unearthed in 1823 after a nun at the Convent of Kechrovounio announced that she had been visited by the Virgin in a dream.

The fact that this first miracle happened at the start of the War of Independence considerably enhanced the shrine's potency. Its importance to the national psyche was re-affirmed in 1940, when on the annual pilgrimage of 15 August an Italian submarine torpedoed and sank a Greek cruiser in the harbour. The two countries were not yet at war, but the incident hardened Greek determination to tolerate no more insults.

Tinos was Venetian for 500 years until 1715, thanks to the virtually impregnable mountain fortress of Exombourgo. The Venetians bequeathed to the island one of the strongest Catholic communities in the Aegean and a passion for keeping doves. The latter practice was one Greek subjects were not allowed to share, which is perhaps why, during the century of Turkish occupation which followed, the Tiniots started building dovecotes with such enthusiasm. These remarkable examples of vernacular architecture are the most striking feature of the often lyrical Tiniot landscape, with its cornfields, leafy villages, some 800 chapels and churches (one doubles as a traffic island, another as a bar), and the bevvies of wheeling white doves returning to one of the estimated 1,300 dovecotes, usually two storeys high, sometimes as big as their owners' houses, with entrances of geometrically arranged slabs of schist. Add the sound of plainsong and an evening sun on their wings and the effect is spine-tingling.

Another post-Venetian skill, although much influenced by the Baroque style, at least when incorporated in buildings, is that of carving marble. This played a signicant role in such prosperity as the island enjoyed in the 18th and 19th centuries, especially in and around the village of Pyrgos, where the trade is still actively pursued. Anyone requiring anything more than the most banal stonework anywhere in Greece today will give serious consideration to a worker who hails from Tinos.

The Venetians, who ruled here from 1207 to 1714, introduced the passion for dove-keeping to Tinos, and dovecotes (above right) *are a striking feature of its fertile landscape. Dio Horia* (above left) *reflects the relative affluence of its spruce villages. The churches, such as this* (opposite) *at Kampos, reflect the Italian past.*

The Tiniots are justly famed throughout Greece for their skill in carving stone, notably marble; and Pyrgos (this page) is the place to see their work. Kechrovounio (opposite) surrounds the twelfth-century convent of the same name. A nun here said she was led to the miraculous icon of Tinos in a dream.

*T*he great icing-sugar church
of Panayia Evangelistria
(these pages) in Tinos town
now houses that sacred icon and
is a major place of pilgrimage.
Its gloomy interior, heavy with
incense, is lit by candles, lamps
and the glitter of fervently
burnished metal.

*The convent of Kechrovounio
(opposite) is a structure of
dazzling white-cell geometry.
As one soon comes to expect of a
Greek village, trees provide shade
and a sense of fruitful ease,
here in Pyrgos (right and below
right), while wood brings a
homely touch to old stone houses.*

THE ARCHITECTURE OF MYKONOS is one of the wonders of the Cyclades. But nobody knows quite how it came about. It is, after all, vernacular, a palimpsest of constructions which just happened without the benefit of architects or any kind of plan. One can seek a logic in its huddle (shortage of space inside the original medieval fortifications) or in its labyrinthine twists and turns (to baffle raiders or the ferocious *meltemi* summer wind) and semi-private courtyards, many with family chapels. Outside staircases, often wooden and brightly painted, give access to the upstairs rooms. A fortuitous arrangement which was to facilitate their rental to modern tourists.

As the jumping-off spot for the sacred island of Delos, on which it was forbidden to spend the night in ancient times, Mykonos must have had an early tourist trade. But it received little mention in antiquity.

It enjoyed a canny mercantile (and maybe piratical) prosperity in the run up to the War of Independence, in which it played a distinguished role. Two of the island's most famous sights, its line of thatched windmills along the ridge of Kato Myli, and the 'captains' houses', with their feet in the water of the Venetia quarter, date from this era. The mills processed corn brought in local ships from surrounding islands, whilst the captains' houses were ideally designed for the clandestine landing and concealment of cargo.

Mykonos' tourist-based modern prosperity began in much the same way as that of Saint-Tropez in France, with artists coming there first, a trickle of painters in the 'thirties, a fashionable bohemian flood in the 'fifties. And it has somehow managed a modern and seemingly accidental miracle to go with its earlier ones. It is very chic, sometimes outrageous, and has perhaps the best restaurants and shops in the land. And yet it remains undeniably a Greek island of blinding afternoons, silent dawns and a full complement of crones, cats, and, it likes to claim, 365 chapels.

Mykonos

Outside staircases originally maximized space in the houses huddled in central Mykonos (opposite), as well as enabling one to be built atop another; today they make it easier to rent upstairs rooms to tourists. The church of Paraportianis (above), where a castle once stood, consists of four interlocking chapels overlooking the surrounding sea.

A dovecote and the characteristic windmills *(above and top) of Mykonos; the familiar geometric dovecote design of schistic rock is sometimes used for the windows of houses and even larger buildings, as seen in this view of the harbour at sunset (right).*

*S*un-dried (and rock-pounded) octopus grilled over
 charcoal is a favourite accompaniment to a
tsipouro *or an* ouzo *aperitif in the Cyclades. Freshly
painted each year, pavements, banisters and steps like
these* (right) *near Tria Pigadia square gleam in the
Mykonos sun, while locally-owned, brightly-painted
boats still predominate in the harbour* (opposite).

Paros

ALTHOUGH much of Paros is dominated by the mountain mass of Profitis Elias (771 metres) it is the rolling mellowness of the surrounding landscape which characterizes the island, especially when compared with the often rugged grandeur of neighbouring Naxos. Paros has long been famed for its marble, especially the now virtually exhausted seam known as *lychnites* which, when appropriately lit, has a translucent glow and was much prized in antiquity. Praxiteles (*fl.* 370-330 B.C.) preferred to work in Parian marble, and its desirability ensured relative prosperity until the end of Venetian rule in the 16th century. The island's olive trees were also destroyed by the departing Venetians; this, coupled with the loss of direct access to the sculptors of Renaissance Italy, was a double blow for Paros and a long period of decline followed.

The long low capital of Parikia is more attractive than it appears at first sight, with its blue domed churches, narrow whitewashed alleys, brightly painted woodwork, and occasional marble door or window frame, nestling around and sometimes incorporated into the remains of the Venetian *kastro* (cannibalizing buildings of a previous era is an art at which Paros has traditionally excelled). This was also the favourite Cycladic haunt of one of the greatest of modern Greeks, George Seferis, the poet, diplomat and Nobel laureate who, according to Lawrence Durrell, claimed that 'the organization of its streets and squares aspired to the condition of music'. But the harbour itself has become the busiest and best connected in all the Greek islands, and although the fabric and for the most part the tranquil dignity of Parikia's centre has been well preserved, a zone of often raucous tourist bars and fast-food restaurants (not even proper Greek ones) has been grafted on to it, whilst the outskirts are consumed in the seemingly endless rush to build ever more accommodation. The contrast with Mykonos, where tourism has been tastefully subsumed into the old town and its life, is striking.

Otherwise, this island has maintained its pride beneath the considerable weight of tourism. Its principal harbour in antiquity was Naoussa, now of little commercial importance and perhaps the prettiest in all the Greek islands. Fishing caiques, chapels, and tavernas, outside which octopi hang to dry, jostle in the animated if nowadays mostly touristic little harbour.

*N*aoussa harbour (left) *was the principal port of Paros in antiquity and remains one of the most picturesque, even if touristic, in the Aegean.*

*T*he villages of Paros (opposite) are classics of Cycladic vernacular
architecture, with outside staircases and rooms arching across
narrow alleyways to maximize living space. The houses only deviate
from the Cycladic norm in rarely having courtyards. Most surfaces get a
fresh coat of whitewash at least once a year. The area around Naoussa
harbour (above), which still has a working fishing fleet, has an almost
gem-like perfection. The harbour itself is guarded by a partly
submerged Venetian fort (left).

*P*lants of Paros: the leaning pylons of the century
plant (Agave americana) (top) *thrive in arid
areas, while the bee orchid (above) prefers a damper
habitat. Lefkes (right) is a calm unspoilt inland
village on an otherwise busy touristic island.*

*N*axos, a fertile and mountainous island, was capital of the
Venetian Duchy of the Aegean in the Middle Ages, and many
Venetian vestiges remain, such as this once grand house (above) *in
the mountain village of Apiranthos and its main square* (opposite).

Naxos

FAMED in antiquity (Theseus jilted Ariadne here,
Dionysos in some versions found the vine) and
beloved by Byron, this is the most majestic of the
Cyclades, with the highest mountain (Zas, or Zeus,
1,000 metres, 3,295 feet), the most prosperous agricultural base and some outstanding architecture.
The old town contains a rare and striking mix of
styles, with the well-preserved walled Kastro of the
Venetians (they regarded this as the capital of their
Aegean possessions) lording it over the more
haphazard and organic Greek town below. Not only
are these two of the finest examples of medieval
defensive planning and vernacular architecture
respectively in Greece, they are also two of the best
documented. The shape of the Greek town, with its
characteristic maze of blind alleys, stubborn alle-
giance to and then sudden swerves away from the
contours, and seeming impossibility of returning
whence you started, was dictated by the terrain,
limited space, and the desire to baffle raiders and
winds alike. But local laws dating from the Turkish
period (the Venetians left in 1536) reveal that this
seemingly chaotic harmony was also governed by
principles constraining the size and right to light of
the houses as well as the dimensions of the streets.

No other island blends the picturesque with the
workaday quite so skilfully. Arrive in Naxos by boat
in the early afternoon, as the principal departures
from Piraeus do, and you will be left in no doubt
that this is still a proper working island. In other
words, it will be closed during the heat of the day
rather than staying open touting for touristic
custom like some of its more flighty neighbours.
Only the restaurants along its agreeable waterfront
will show much sign of life. The island's interior is
one of wild mountain grandeur, prosperous little
villages, magical meadows and olive groves all redolent with farm smells. It can be surprising to learn
that Naxos grows the finest potatoes in Greece, less
so to hear that it is also famed for fruit and corn.
Apiranthos, its most beautiful village, also owes its
present form to Venetians, having been rebuilt in
the 14th century by the Sommaripa and Crispi
dukes. Its modern inhabitants are among the many
mountain Naxiots who trace their origins to Crete
and are talented musicians and versifiers. Coastal
Naxos, alas, is well endowed with those most characteristic of modern Greek structures: the unfinished
and seemingly abandoned reinforced concrete
block, bristling with exposed iron rods.

*T*he capital's Venetian Kastro (far left and left) *might be an outstanding example of medieval defensive planning, but it was also designed for living in, a maze that tempts the explorer as defily as it once frustrated the invader.*

The huge stone portal that has become the iconic symbol of Naxos (opposite) is all that remains of the ancient temple to Apollo which once dominated the harbour. An architectural oddity of Naxos is its scattering of Maniot-style tower houses (above) built in the 17th and 18th centuries, when windmills such as this ruined one (left) near Apiranthos would have ground their owners' corn. The thirteenth-century Catholic cathedral (below) was restored in the nineteen-fifties.

*A*piranthos viewed from the east
(above) *looks exactly the
same as in the earliest photograph
from this spot. The curve of the
outer wall of this little chapel
(right), also in Apiranthos, throws
the rugged texture of adjacent
stonework into sharp relief. The
Kastro (opposite) still conveys a
sense of great defensive strength.*

Sifnos

DESPITE or just possibly because of its relative obscurity (few people who don't know Greece have ever heard of Sifnos), this is one of the most remarkable of the Greek islands.

In the first place it was rich. Its now long abandoned gold and silver mines had made the islanders the wealthiest in Greece by the 6th century B.C., Herodotus records. By the 1st century B.C. Sifniot pottery had become the community's most successful export. This has been through several cycles of boom and bust since then, but for much of the 200 years until the middle of this century it was again one of the island's chief claims to fame. Its heat-resistant qualities were particularly prized, hence the number of often eccentric home-made chimney pots you will see on the island. Many houses incorporate examples of local ceramics in their walls.

And then there are its cooks. When I first asked a taxi-driver in Athens to take me to the Sifnos boat his immediate reaction was: 'Ah, you are going to meet the best cooks in Greece.' He was right. There ensued an elsewhere unremarkable, but in the islands quite improbable, succession of dishes, such as pork cooked in wine, mushrooms and herbs, a rabbit stew, freshly cooked beetroot, spicy vegetarian spaghettis, sloshing copper jugs of country wine, and unforgettable breakfasts under the trees on the Kamares waterfront, with mouth-watering concoctions of yoghurt, fruit, nuts and honey, fresh fruit juice, eggs and crispy bacon, espresso coffee, what you will. All enough to make you want to sharply re-educate the next waiter on the next Greek island who brings rusks, luke-warm water, a sachet of instant coffee and some evaporated milk and calls it breakfast.

But then it seems the Sifniots simply don't want to be like everyone else. Instead of having a *skala* (Kamares) and a *hora*, they have three *horas*. Kastro on its dramatic clifftop perch was the capital from ancient times until the War of Independence when the mantle passed to Apollonia, a short downhill walk from its sibling in fact and dedication (to Apollo and Artemis respectively), the more affluent Artemonas.

Kastro owes its present form to the Venetians: a defensive ring of cramped houses in a nervous medieval huddle presenting only windows and dovecotes to the outer world the better to protect the inner town with its often vaulted alleys and less gloomy and more substantial dwellings, many of which have been whitewashed so often over the centuries that the accretions now seem softened.

The view from the belfry of Panayia Kohi church in Artemonas (opposite)*, the most elegant of Sifnos' three* horas*; a stairway* (above) *links it to that of Apollonia. This corner of Vathi* (left) *is typical of the island's most beautiful seaside village.*

*S*ifnos has always been famed
for its pottery (above). It is
particularly prized for its heat-
resistant properties, hence the
island's fine line in eccentric
home-made chimney pots. Vathi
(right) *is one of the most lovely
bays in the Cyclades, with the
tiny monastery of the Archangel
Gabriel next to the tavernas on a
sandy beach. Until recently there
was no road to Vathi, and much
of the island is still linked by
marble-paved mule trails across
its terraced landscape* (opposite).

WE DON'T KNOW much about Sikinos, which has traditionally been one of the more compelling reasons for going there. Though scarcely mentioned in antiquity, it has the remains of a seemingly once impressive Roman mausoleum, now a church, for which the most likely explanation is that this was the final resting-place of an eminent and troublesome exile. Like most places on Sikinos a long hike is needed to get there.

The island was probably uninhabited when the forebears of the present occupants arrived, usually described as sixteenth-century refugees from Ottoman Crete, though Crete was not then Turkish and the Cyclades were. Not that there is any reason to believe that the Turks concerned themselves with Sikinos when it was their nominal fiefdom any more than did the Venetians before them. Not the least of the rum things about this dry, uncompromising, end-of-the-line kind of island is that the newcomers built their capital on twin peaks. The higher one is called Hora (the usual name of the place where everyone lives), while the real heart of the place is the lower one, Kastro (normally the name applied to a fortified peak too remote for everyday life).

Ferries were unable to dock here until the early 'nineties. There is only one road, up to Kastro down to Skala, as Alapronia (at least) is conventionally called. A bus, which otherwise rarely stirs itself, meets the ferry which, as well as foot passengers, disgorges the odd lorry creaking with provisions, but scarcely a car. There might be only one road but the old mule tracks remain in good repair and the striking thing about Sikinos is not the sight of the odd old man riding by which, after all, is still a common enough if fast-disappearing sight in other communities. It is that of entire mule or donkey trains driven not by old men but by strapping young bloods with rampant black moustaches: muleteers with swash and buckle, manifest old-style Cretans, fit to eat the pasha's men for breakfast. Kastro itself has a sparse, lofty tranquillity, not a place to be stuck in during bad weather in winter; apart from anything else, there are no restaurants. Even in summer everything can be closed by 10 p.m. (when on more sophisticated islands locals will just be sitting down to eat). But its slow, sad tumbling-down has been put hesitantly into reverse by improved communications and some tourism.

Sikinos

The neat landscape of a remote island (opposite), Sikinos, a former place of political exile, has few motor vehicles or tourist facilities and we know little of its history. The church of Pantanassa dominates the main square of Kastro (above): Cycladic from the paving stones to its bells.

*D*efensive spots come no better than a hill with a water supply. The fortified monastery of Zoodohou Pygis ('spring of life'), now gently decaying above Kastro (left), would have been named for the spring it enclosed. It was a place of refuge for islanders during pirate raids. In Kastro itself (below) houses faced inwards for protection though, as with this eighteenth-century doorway (below right), decorative elements were not overlooked.

*E*nigmatic Episkopi (above): a Roman temple transformed into a Christian church and then a monastery. Was it once the burial vault of some Roman political exile? This remote spot is thought to have once been the island's capital. Donkeys (left) and mules are still the only means of transport, save along the couple of miles of the Skala-Hora road.

Santorini

THIRA, also known as Santorini or, in ancient times, Kalliste ('most beautiful'), is perhaps the most remarkable sight in the whole Mediterranean, the remains of the greatest volcanic explosion in history. In around 1500 B.C., with about three times the force of Krakatoa, the centre of the island was blown away in a cataclysm which would have rained debris on much of the eastern Mediterranean and sent tidal waves as far as Spain. It is likely that this played a part in the roughly contemporaneous downfall of Minoan civilization in nearby Crete, entirely plausible that this was the factual basis of the story of the destruction of Atlantis, whilst more versatile theories also find an echo of the eruption in Ulysses' encounter with floating islands (which would have been Thiran pumice) and the waters of the Red Sea parting to facilitate the flight of Moses and the children of Israel (it was not the Red Sea, according to this hypothesis, but a Mediterranean lagoon system which emptied as the sea drew in prior to expelling the tidal wave).

What is beyond doubt is that Thira itself was the seat of a glittering Minoan subculture and that all that was left was a 32-square-mile crater (*caldera*) some 1,250 feet deep into which the sea rushed (this implosion and subsequent explosions causing the tidal waves), with the remnants of the island towering almost as high again in near sheer cliffs above the waters. Up to several hundred feet of ash buried any remains of contemporary life for over 3,000 years.

Arriving in the *caldera* by ship is a breathtaking experience. The volcano still smoulders in the sinister jumble of black rock inching itself up from beneath the sea to create the island of Nea Kameni. The town perches dizzily along the striated cliffs high above; with natural defences like these there is no need for the usual Cycladic huddle. But were it not for tourism it would probably have fallen into disrepair by now; the last shaking the volcano gave it, in 1956, seemed terminal. It was remote, had no airport, no road (let alone today's cable-car) up from

the harbour, and no real means of support, in short, the sort of place Greek governments of those days thought of only when wondering where to dispose of political exiles. But frankly tourism has also turned the capital, somewhat confusingly written as Fira (or even Phira), into something of a theme-park through which cruise-ship passengers are shifted and their pockets lightened with great speed. The village of Ia is the better place from which to contemplate the awesome beauty of this island.

The volcano has touched every aspect of life, not all of it for the worse. The soil is fertile, if short of water; the landscape away from the sheer sides of the *caldera* is a picture of tranquillity as it slopes towards the sea proper with its black volcanic beaches. And among the mineral riches rained down by the volcano were copious quantities of pozzuolana, much prized, especially in the pre-reinforced concrete age, for the ease with which it could be quarried and subsequently mixed with slaked lime into a strong and highly water-resistant form of cement plaster. It was the strength of this material which enabled local builders to span openings of up to four metres with barrel vaults (on many other islands a two-metre limit was effectively imposed on vernacular building by the length of the cypress-like Phoenician juniper of the island *garrigue*).

The malleability of this material gives local houses their soft, rounded, almost sculpted look. It was quarrying for pozzuolana for the construction of the Suez Canal in the last century which first revealed that there were Minoan settlements with breathtaking artwork wondrously preserved in its stifling embrace. The island enjoyed a brief burst of maritime prosperity in the first half of the last century, and some substantial Neoclassical (Italianate) houses date from that era. Note also the local use of black basaltic paving stones (*plakota*). Sunset is the time to contemplate the kaleidoscopic view across the *caldera* from Ia, as swallows swirl and skirl below.

*P*erhaps the most remarkable sight in the Mediterranean: the caldera of Santorini, the result of a massive volcanic explosion around 1500 B.C., is best viewed from the village of Ia (left) or from the deck of an arriving ship.

*L*iving on the edge of a volcano: houses and churches in Ia (this page) *have evolved their own kind of sturdy grace. The vaulted roofs and curving, almost sculpted, lines of the houses* (opposite) *were made possible by copious local supplies of pozzuolana, a volcanic ash which, until the advent of reinforced concrete, was one of the most versatile and highly-prized building materials.*

*T*he fertile volcanic soil of Santorini (overleaf left) *produces good if limited crops (not least the grapes for a worthwhile wine) and presents a contrasting landscape of pastoral tranquillity as it slopes away from the* caldera *to the island's outer coast. The Sphinx is not an ancient sculpture* (overleaf right), *but it adds an appropriate air of mystery to the view across the waters of a once mighty volcano.*

Other Aegean Islands

*T*he rest of the Aegean has tended to have
wealthier, better defended islands, to have more
legacies of the post-Byzantine occupying power (Italian
or Turk) and be more involved in trade and shipping
(the Turks let them sail under the flag of their Russian
Orthodox co-religionaries) than the Cyclades.

Chios, for instance, has many substantial Genoese
country mansions in the fertile Kampos plain (the Genoese
stayed on Chios till 1566). But the real stars here are the
wealthy mastic villages of Pyrgos (with striking sgraffito
wall decorations) and Mesta. And nothing comes Greeker
than the monastery of Nea Moni up in the hills, with its
world-class mosaics and its ossuary with neat Turkish
sword holes in the skulls. (Turkey is a brooding presence
on the Chiot horizon.)

These islands have many arkontika *(loosely
translating as 'mansion') houses built by merchant
families, usually in the last century. Those in Halki, for
instance, have floors made from the now forgotten but
once much-prized, broad (15-inch) 'St. Petersburg'
planking; the plaster is* porcelana, *smooth and hard like
ostrich-egg shell and made from volcanic ash by a lost
recipe (if anyone finds it the mayor would like it back).*

But our subdivisions are not architecturally exclusive.
The Cyclades (notably Sifnos) have the odd cluster of
arkontika *houses. The rest of the Aegean has its share
of white cuboid architecture, notably Astypalea (which,
but for a slip of a treaty writer's pen, should have been
Cycladic), Patmos, and Lindos on Rhodes, with its
acropolis, ancient Greek temple, sandy bay, white houses,
cobbled paths and courtyards (and, it should be said,
more than its fair share of visitors).*

Lindos on Rhodes (opposite), *seen from its acropolis.*

The Dodecanese

THE DODECANESE, sometimes referred to as the southern
Sporades, translates as the 'twelve islands,' though by any
count there are at least fourteen. Like the 'seven islands' of the
Ionian they had a common history prior to becoming part of
modern Greece, the last islands to do so, in 1947. The name
first seems to have gained official currency when Suleiman the
Magnificent granted twelve islands off the coast of Asia Minor
trading privileges in the 16th century (though the Byzantine
chronicler Theophanes had used the term seven centuries
earlier). Compared with the often more or less forgotten and
remote Cyclades it was their good fortune to become
prosperous, their misfortune to be coveted for this and for
their strategic position offshore from the mainland. In 1912,
after a brief war with Turkey, Italy took the Dodecanese
(which corresponded roughly with the original twelve) and
held them until the British liberated them at the end of World
War II, transferring them to Greece on 7 March 1947.

Despite their belated unification with modern Greece,
these and other islands down the coast of present-day Turkey
(notably Chios and Lesbos) were very much at the centre of
the ancient Greek world. Prior to the rise of Athens they, along
with mainland settlements opposite, constituted Ionia, set the
pace for the development of the city-state and led the Greek
world in the arts, notably poetry and sculpture. During the
Middle Ages, the Genoese (rather than the Venetians) had a
strong presence in (and occasional possession of) these islands.

The villages of the eastern Aegean tend to show more
evidence of urban planning than those of the Cyclades, and
their houses are more likely to have tiled roofs.

Patmos

'I JOHN...was on an island called Patmos...and I heard behind me a loud voice like a trumpet saying, "Write what you see in a book and send it to the seven churches"...' Thus St. John the Divine's account of how he came to write *The Book of Revelation*. Whether or not he was the same person as John the Apostle, and whether the event which began with the heart-stopping words, 'I am the Alpha and the Omega', took place in the very grotto which is today pointed out in the Monastery of the Apocalypse midway between the Skala and Hora is relatively unimportant. Just the fact that the Revelation by the author's own account took place and the book was written on Patmos explains all that is so striking about the place today.

Above all, there is the fortress-monastery, majestic, potent, which seems to have sprung ready formed and eternal from the rock, without the usual antecedent palimpsest (though Orestes, fleeing the Furies after killing his mother, is said to have built a placatory temple to Artemis here). In fact, 1,000 years elapsed after the events described, until in 1088 one Christodoulos, something of a warrior monk, was granted permission by the Byzantine emperor to build the Monastery of St. John atop its hill.

Possibly uniquely among major constructions in the Aegean, it has survived nine turbulent centuries effectively intact, its dark, almost windowless walls lowering over the encircling white of the houses of Hora, the power of its legend and its monks warding off unseemly developments on the island to this day. Despite a massive influx of cruise-ship passengers, over 150,000 of whom make the pilgrimage up from Skala to enter the monastery each year, Patmos has been spared the greater excesses of contemporary tourism. Having no airport helps.

In recent years wealthy outsiders have bought houses in Hora, turning it into something of a ghetto of good taste. Skala, where most of local life goes on, dates no further back than the 19th century, before which it appears to have been much favoured as a port of call by corsairs. Hence, no doubt, the circumspection with which the monks built their home.

*T*he massive defensive walls of the Monastery of
St. John, seemingly immune to the passing
centuries, lour over the Hora of Patmos (opposite)
with its attendant chapels. Wealthy incomers have
helped preserve Patmos' peaceful charms (this page).

Halki

Halki had a brief flowering towards the end of the last century. With piracy suppressed and its sponge trade booming, profits were ploughed back into some splendid little Neoclassical houses around the compact harbour. Many have recently been restored, initially with Unesco and European Union funding, later by tour operators, to provide tourist accommodation. In their rooms you may find floors made with the now virtually forgotten and unobtainable 'St. Petersburg' boards, a massive 15 inches wide, and walls painted eggshell with *porcelana*, which was made, nobody today quite knows how, from volcanic dust (the mayor would dearly love the recipe back to assist in restoration). For some reason, the regional collapse of the sponge trade, and hence the dilapidation of these houses, is attributed in Halki to a virus attacking the delicate submarine plants, as a result of which, again uniquely, Halki's spongers seem to have decamped almost as one to a single destination, Tarpon Springs in Florida. Tarpon Springs Boulevard, which runs somewhat forlornly from the village past the beach towards the old (abandoned) and castle-capped hill village of Horio, is a tangible reminder of this diaspora, and indeed was donated by its members. The landscape viewed from Horio is harsh and dry, vibrant only with heat, the outlines of long abandoned fields and estates still faintly visible.

The people of Halki, once wealthy from sponge-diving, built some impressive houses around their harbour (opposite) in the last century. Many are now being rescued from disrepair by international agencies and tour operators. In such harsh and dry terrain only prickly pear (above) flourishes unaided. This black and white pebble mosaic outside the little church of Ag Nikolas (right) is a simple but effective decoration and a hallmark characteristic of Rhodes and its satellite islands.

Nissyros

THE DOMINANT FACT of life here is the still hissing but dormant volcano at its heart. Five hundred years ago, before its last major eruption, the island had a 1,400-metre peak. Now it is but half that height and the vast Stefanos crater which was created by the explosion has become something of a tourist attraction. There, you may sit in a café and listen to the hissing and groaning which legend attributes to a giant, one Polyvotis, imprisoned under the earth by Poseidon. The village of Nikia is stunningly situated near the edge of the *caldera*, close to one of the island's many hot springs. Its inhabitants make a sweet, non-alcoholic almond drink, *soumada*.

The islanders are a spirited bunch and recently saw off the state electricity company which had been experimenting with geothermal power in a high-handed way. They are also modestly prosperous. Gypsum and pumice quarrying, mostly on the satellite island of Yiali, have provided a steady income in the past, and the volcanic soil is fertile. Outside the desolation of the *caldera*, this is a surprisingly green and fruitful island.

Mandraki, one of the region's cheerier harbours, is overlooked by two fortresses: a Crusader one with the added curiosity of a monastery with an underground chapel (the Panayia Spiliana), and another of great antiquity about which little is known. Day-trippers from Kos provide the bulk of the island's tourist income.

Income from gypsum quarrying and remittances from emigrants in New York keep the villages of Nissyros spruce and proud. Nikia (right) is close to the edge of a volcanic crater which has become the island's chief tourist attraction.

*T*he village of Emborio, with its pristine little church (above), *is enjoying something of a revival as Athenians and foreigners buy houses here; some residents have hot water piped direct from the volcano. Complex dry stone walls, a nationalist graffito and an unusual roof design, probably to maximize water catchment, outside Nikia* (opposite), *contrast with the more classic street geometry of Nikia itself* (right).

*T*he *'round' square of Nikia, with its classic use of pebble patterned cobbles, the village's quietly embellished buildings* (right and above), *and the Emborio church* (top) *embody the solid thriftiness of the Greek island peoples.*

The citizens of Symi made their first fortunes from shipbuilding and sponge-diving and built beautiful, often Neoclassical houses in Horio (right) from which they were able to look down on one of the most perfect little harbours in the Aegean (opposite).

Symi

A FEW MILES from the Turkish mainland, Symi was not so long ago a wealthy and populous little island, famed for its wooden ships and sponge divers. But the shipbuilders consumed its forests, and by the end of their efforts in the early nineteenth-century struggle for independence (which Symi itself and its neighbours did not then achieve) it was the more or less naked but dazzlingly beautiful island one still sees today.

Further economic decline followed the Italian occupation in this century. The island's previous trading links with the mainland were severed, while the islanders of Kalymnos seized the initiative in the sponge trade, or what little remained of it after the invention of synthetic substitutes.

The once elegant little capital, which is divided into Yialos, the harbour area, and Horio above (linked by some splendid mule-sized cobbled stairways and all capped by a Crusader castle built by the Knights of St. John), was in decline for much of this century, its beautiful Neoclassical merchant houses and warehouses falling into disrepair. Perhaps the cruellest blow came in 1945 when the retreating Germans blew up their ammunition dump, wrecking much of Horio. Allied bombing also damaged the harbour area.

Happily, tourism has been good to Symi and reversed its seemingly terminal decline, particularly since 1974 when the Turkish invasion of Cyprus led to Symi replacing the Turkish mainland as the preferred destination for excursion boats bearing escapees from the uninspiring resorts of Rhodes. Lacking an airport, sandy beaches and supplies of water, it was never itself at risk from the excesses of mass tourism, and once the day-trip invasion has departed it reverts to being a small and homogeneous community with a lively café society. Many a discerning traveller would holiday nowhere else.

The island's plentiful though often legally encumbered stock of old and abandoned houses is being gradually restored as tourist accommodation. The ground-floor warehouses which were a feature of many harbour houses now function as the hub of evening activity in their new incarnations as bars and restaurants. As the wonderful 450-step Kali Strata (Beautiful Way), with its Neoclassical mansions, gradually recovers its former glory, Symi today, now a conservation area, its houses piled high around it in a natural mountain amphi-theatre, is one of the most beautiful and stylish little harbours in the Aegean, an engaging haunt for all who love the essential spirit of the islands.

*T*hough sponges are still on sale in Symi (right)
they are probably imported, while the tourists
who buy them are the source of the island's renewed
prosperity. Magnificent stairways (above) link the
harbour of Yialos with the houses above, many of
which have been restored as tourist accommodation.
Working fishing boats and their crews (opposite)
still have their place in Symi's stylish mix.

*T*he clean elegance of Horio's buildings is punctuated by the deep
green cylinder of a cypress (opposite). Italianate architraves and
cornices (above and left) contrast with the very Greek church of the
Assumption of the Virgin above the village (above left).

*M*astic, a versatile form of vegetable gum, brought Chios great wealth in the Middle Ages. Pyrgi, largest of the two main mastic villages (these pages), was fortified by the Genoese and is particularly notable for the 'xysta' (also spelled 'ksysta') decoration of many exterior walls, a geometric style achieved by superimposing two colours and then scraping one away as in the Renaissance Italian 'sgrafitto' process. Tomatoes strung like beads dry in the sun (left) against a backdrop of typically exuberant embellishment.

Chios

Chios is an island of substance: a proud, cultured, mercantile community which, with its dependent islands of Inousses and Psara, owns fifty per cent of the Greek mercantile marine. Many villagers flit between here and America; the man at the next table could be worth over a billion dollars, especially if his name is Livanos, while the vessel resting in the next cove is as likely to be an oil tanker as it is a wooden caique.

Chios owes the original source of its wealth, possibly its name, and certainly that of its most impressive villages, to a tree which was once cultivated nowhere else on earth save in the southern part of this island. The mastic tree, a variant of the lentisk, produces a resin which, when used as a chewing-gum, had breath-sweetening, relaxing and digestive properties much valued by the Turks, who granted the island special trading privileges as a result. It was also used in picture varnish and to flavour liqueurs.

Are the Greeks a literary people? You will see them in cafés devouring newspapers as voraciously as any nation. Yet a Greek reading a book is a rare sighting indeed. But at least they started it and Chios has the best of several rival claims to be the home of Homer, and was second only to Athens in ancient times as a centre of literary excellence. Throughout the Middle Ages, when the Turks pragmatically left local affairs to the Greeks and the remnants of an earlier Genoese aristocracy to arrange, it was as famed for its learning as it was for its wealth and elegance. Adamantios Korais, founder in 1792 of the library here which still bears his name, virtually reinvented modern (demotic) Greek single-handed as a written language, managing to make it correspond with the tongue spoken in the villages, while at the same time remaining a close and indisputable descendant of ancient written Greek.

All this came to a terrible end in 1822. Incensed by what they saw as treachery in joining the independence struggle, the Turks slaughtered or enslaved most of Chios's inhabitants, sparing only those of the *mastikhoria* (the mastic villages). The senseless brutality and extent of the massacre (25,000 is the lowest estimate of the dead) was widely credited with swinging European opinion behind the independence struggle. Delacroix's potent painting of it, now in the Louvre, encapsulates European pain and outrage. Alas, what the Turks began, nature finished. In 1881 an earthquake devastated much of what remained of Chiot elegance, though some notable Genoese great houses and orchards survive in the Kampos valley, one of the few places in the Greek islands where the sound of running water is a familiar one.

Ironically, the resultant diasporas shifted the balance of economic power in Chios. Those who emigrated or sought their fortunes at sea prospered (Chiot shipowners have always favoured local crews), while the mastic trade and the otherwise intact mastic villages went into a relative decline which was halted in recent years only by a modest influx of tourism. Due to their prosperity (and, doubtless, lack of beaches) the other villages have never been ardent pursuers of the tourist drachma.

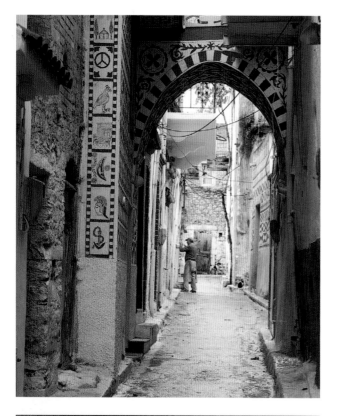

*T*he mastic villages were built as composite defensive entities under the Genoese in the 14th and 15th centuries. Archways across the maze of streets (this page) *not only maximized space by creating extra rooms and provided mutual buttressing in the event of earthquake, they also served as hidden passageways via which the inhabitants could outflank any attackers who may have penetrated the perimeter walls. Sorting the mastic resin from other debris (opposite) is a time-consuming but no longer economically important chore.*

*H*ad the history of Chios been as well recorded
as that of Renaissance Italy then a name as
illustrious as that of Giotto might have come down
to us from the hilltop monastery of Nea Moni. For
here, a hand or hands unknown working in the 11th
century bequeathed us mosaics which were living,
moving portraits two to three centuries before the
Italians achieved the same effect (above). The
inhabitants of the monastery (opposite), now a
nunnery where clocks run on Byzantine time, did
not escape the events of 1822. An ossuary contains
piles of skulls, some with chillingly neat sword
holes in their temples.

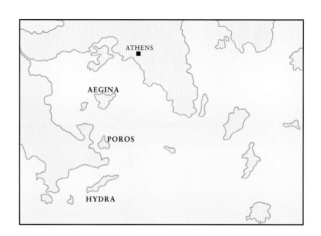

The Argo-Saronic Islands

THE ARGO-SARONIC ISLANDS, trailing south from Piraeus through the Saronic Gulf and into the Argolic one, often seem from a distance to blend into the mainland mountains of the nearby Argolid. These are the most accessible of the Greek islands, linked with each other and Piraeus by fast and frequent boat services. One, Salamina, is virtually in the (nowadays alas polluted) maw of Piraeus. Better known abroad by its ancient name of Salamis, the waters between it and the mainland were the scene of a famous victory when, in 480 B.C., the Athenian fleet trounced a Persian one three times its size.

Most of the islands of this group have at some point in their history been notable naval powers, placed as they are right at the nautical crossroads of Greece, navigated through or called at by eminent travellers, traders, and expeditionaries back to Theseus and into the mists of legend. Ernle Bradford, in his classic work, *The Greek Islands,* goes so far as to write that, 'More than anywhere on the mainland, more than Athens herself, these waters are at the heart of Greece.'

In Turkish times these islands enjoyed a high degree of autonomy, but (or possibly because) they were also fertile recruiting grounds for the Turkish navy.

The island of Poros is an echo of the mainland mountains opposite, its waters redolent of Greek naval history.

Aegina

Itinerant vendors have long served even the most remote Greek communities. Today in sophisticated Aegina the canny shopper knows that the brightly painted fruit and vegetable caiques (above) *in the lively tree-shaded harbour* (opposite) *still offer the best value for money.*

AEGINA is something of a commuter island, being only forty minutes by hydrofoil from Piraeus. It was, for a brief, glorious moment and in recognition of the contribution of its fleet to the struggle, the first capital of the then but partly liberated modern Greece in the 1820s. It was also, in ancient times, the first Greek city-state to mint coins, an indication of its great antiquity as a centre of culture.

With its elegant workaday little harbour, it remains all that the Greeks themselves find most attractive in their own land (they are not as drawn to the stark simplicity of the Cyclades): octopus sizzles on charcoal grills at the entry of vine-covered *psaro-tavernas* (fish restaurants) in leafy back alleys. There is a vibrant fish market (though fish are fast becoming an endangered species in Greek waters), some wonderful coffee houses, cornucopian food shops burnished with time, and caiques bobbing in the harbour sell vegetables to passing shoppers. Nikos Kazantzakis had a home in Aegina where he wrote *Zorba the Greek* during the German occupation. 'From the moment I set foot in Aegina', he wrote, 'I've become another man. Exhilaration, almost happiness, sea, solitude, there is no more perfect climate for my spirit.'

The straits of Poros (left) *seen from the island; ferries scuttle back and forth across the narrow divide. Even in the confined space of Poros' streets, house-owners manage to create wonderfully dense and brilliant gardens* (right) *with just a few pots, a pergola and a roof terrace. It is the passionate disregard for form or formality in the Greek garden that often creates so dazzling an effect.*

Poros

COMPACT POROS, vibrant in summer with pleasure craft and ferries crossing the narrow band of sea which separates it from the mainland, has a more solid past than immediate appearances might suggest. In the 7th century B.C., and then known as Kalauria, it headed the Kalaurian League, which included Athens and was the dominant naval power of the region. There has long been a sanctuary to Poseidon near the island's highest point. The Athenian orator and democrat Demosthenes took poison here (rather than face capture by his Macedonian enemies) in 322 B.C. Pausanius paid homage to his tomb in the temple enclosure some five centuries later. Nearly two millennia on, the Protocol of Poros (1828), wherein the 'great powers' of Britain, France and Russia settled the basis of the new Greek nation, was hammered out here. Not long after that, in a typically Greek episode of intemperate defiance, Admiral Miaoulis fired the finest ships of his revolutionary fleet in Poros harbour rather than deliver them to Russian command. The glorious naval tradition continued: Greece's first naval arsenal was and its premier naval training college still is on Poros.

It is possible to read Henry Miller and wonder whether he made a mistake when he wrote in an oft-quoted passage from *The Colossus of Maroussi* that, 'To sail slowly through the streets of Poros is to recapture the joy of passing through the neck of the womb. It is a joy almost too deep to be remembered.' Surely he meant sailing through 'the straits of Poros'? Well, yes and no. The fact that we are confused is, as his friend Lawrence Durrell implies in a later piece of his own, a tribute to the special nature and geography of Poros, its waterfront houses and cafés so close both to the sea and to the mainland opposite that they seem to enjoy an intimate relationship with passing sea traffic. It is indeed a very good spot to sit and savour island Greece. Even if that passing traffic is nowadays almost entirely touristic and the Poros so beloved of Miller much changed.

*W*hite, geometric, precise but softened by foliage and a calm sea, a Poros house with a view (left); a practical metal gate opens on the cool mystery of an island house (above). Many island men, especially of the older generation, have second lives on their boats, a cool refuge towards the end of a summer day (below left). The kiosk or periptero (below) is a venerable Greek institution. As timeless as the kiosk is the four-square taverna table (opposite) with chequered cloth and rush-bottomed chairs.

Hydra

BEAUTIFUL HYDRA is at first sight all one could hope for in a Greek village: a string of donkeys, some hopeful cats, and perhaps one of the island's couple of municipally owned and only motor vehicles waiting at the water's edge of the perfectly curved inner harbour, while a traditional caique unloads the necessities of life. Grand houses built by eighteenth- and nineteenth-century shipping fortunes line the harbour along which on summer weekend evenings one of the most fashionable *voltas* in Greece unfolds, while behind it all a wonderfully stark and towering amphitheatrical rockscape speckled white with chapels fulfills all one's hopes and expectations as to how a proper Greek island should look. It is magnificent. But it is not quite as it appears.

Hydra's fortunes in antiquity have gone largely unrecorded, which suggests that they were unremarkable, but by the beginning of the 19th century it had joined its better chronicled neighbours in owning a substantial merchant fleet (blockade-running Russian grain to France during the Napoleonic wars had been a Hydriot speciality). Like them, it played a heroic naval role in the War of Independence. And then, partly through exhaustion from its efforts, partly because the age of steam required a coal-bunkering station with a larger harbour, it lost its dominance of Aegean shipping to Syros and Piraeus.

In the 'fifties Hydra was discovered by film-makers (*Boy on a Dolphin* with Sophia Loren was shot here) and by the fashionable bohemian crowd. At about the same time the islanders, sensing that tourists would soon be following, seem to have made a very intelligent decision. It was, essentially, to preserve the film set. On an island virtually devoid of such basic mass-tourist essentials as beaches (let alone beach-front space to build on) and water, this was clearly quick-thinking at a time when the rest of the Mediterranean was rushing to put up concrete hotels and beach umbrellas. And they succeeded brilliantly, perhaps too brilliantly. Hydra today, especially by day, positively groans under the weight of tourists in general and day-trippers in particular. Listed as a protected monument by the Council of Europe, it still looks much as it must have done one hundred years ago (though doubtless cleaner and better painted). But it is a luxury that only tourism, its only industry, allows it to afford.

Such vulgarities as private cars, modern buildings and an airport have been kept at bay by the Hydriots; as a result, their film-set harbour remains as busy as it is beautiful.

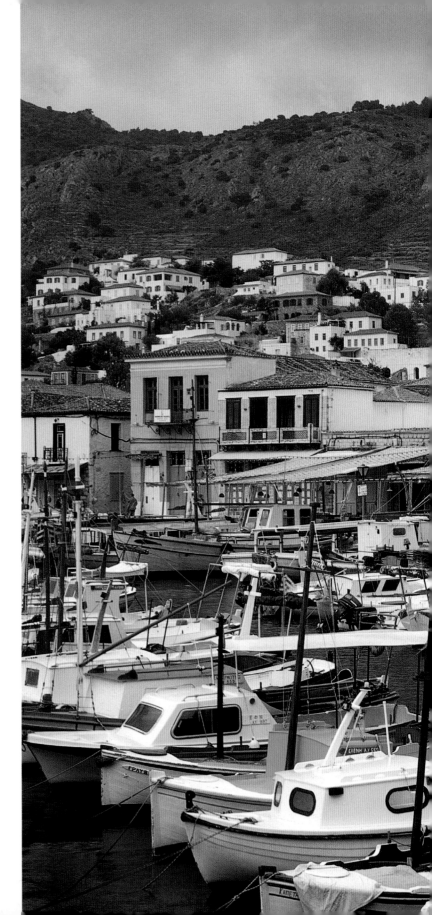

*T*he Hydra waterfront by night (opposite): *a stylish place to stroll as tavernas trail reflections in the water. These* boats (above) *seem to be drawn to the harbour in an unconscious geometry rather than to be attached to it.*

The Ionian Islands

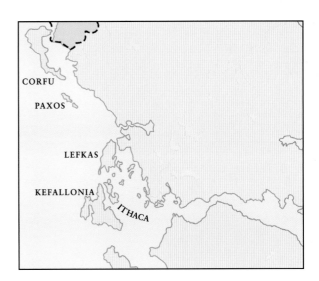

THE IONIAN SEA, with the Ionian Islands, lies between the toe of Italy and the Peloponnese. It is not the same place as ancient Ionia, which was along the shores of present-day Turkey.

Until very recently, the main islands which, with their attendant satellites, were regarded as Ionian numbered seven, and indeed were called the 'Eftanissa', or 'seven islands', by the Greeks. But then the odd one out, far-flung Kythira off the southernmost tip of the Peloponnese, which had very little in common with the other six save an accident or two of history, was regrouped with the Argo-Saronic islands and Piraeus in a local government boundary change, leaving just six.

The Ionian Islands (with the exception of Lefkas) alone of modern Greece was never Turkish. Instead, after passing back and forth between sundry Crusader ('Frankish') hands from the 11th century onwards, as western Europeans idly dismembered the Byzantine state, the islands finally ended up with Venice.

For four centuries thereafter, until the Serene Republic itself fell to Napoleon in 1797, the Ionian Islands were thus both Venetian and for much of that time the furthest outpost of the Christian West, separated only by a narrow stretch of water from the hostile Ottoman shore, as great and perilous a divide in its time as ever the Iron Curtain was to be, and far more enduring. Its legacy still haunts the Greeks. A British protectorate over the islands followed the downfall of Napoleon, until they were ceded to the infant Greek nation in 1864. This British episode did much to open a window on Greece for western philhellenism.

Much of the distinctive architecture of the Ionian (save that of Corfu) was destroyed by the earthquake of 1953. It flattened Zakynthos town, which under its Italian name of Zante had for centuries been hymned as 'the flower of the Levant'. But the cultural undercurrents, the cuisine (with specialities such as *sofrito* or *bourdetto*) and the music (with the mandolin performing the function of the *bouzouki*) remain Italianate in these islands to this day, just as the second language, at least for older people, is also Italian.

The Ionian offers easier sailing than the Aegean and is popular with flotillas, much to the approval of hopeful cats in Lakka on Paxos (opposite).

Even the Ionian landscape contrives to remain oddly Italianate. Its winter rainfall, high compared with that of the Aegean, renders the islands relatively lush and green, with cypress trees, particularly vigorous in their southwards spread during the last fifty years, adding a dark dignity to the countryside, while the stately old olive trees of Corfu and Paxos in particular, whose planting the Venetians subsidized, and which have never been severely pruned or worked like modern ones, create chivalric groves.

Inevitably, the cultural differences between the Ionian and the rest of Greece are eliding. Tourism has added an intriguing twist to the process, in that quite a few Aegean and Levantine items, from the *bouzouki* to *taramasalata*, from *yiros* to *houmous*, all of which were relatively unknown in the Ionian a generation or so ago, have been imported not as one might expect direct from the rest of Greece so much as via western Europe, whose tourists (particularly the British whose concepts of Greekness owe much to Cypriot restaurateurs and *Zorba*) expect to find such things there. But it was always the very accessibility both culturally and geographically of the Ionian in general, and Corfu in particular, which made it the first mass-tourist destination in Greece for western Europeans. The Greeks have long shared a peculiar and revealing (if finally fading) mental block with the British in that they talk of 'going to Europe'. The Ionians alone do not. They regard themselves as there already.

The islands have virtually no classical remains, and few pre- Roman associations. The kingdom of Odysseus (Ulysses) was here, and so probably were most of the places he visited in the *Odyssey*. But precise geographic locations continue to elude us. Later, in 664 B.C., it saw the first recorded naval battle in history in which Corfu saw off a fleet from Corinth which was attempting to reimpose colonial rule. A later sea battle between the two city states, that in 433 B.C. off Syvota on the mainland opposite Corfu, was to precipitate the Peloponnesian war.

Corfu

CORFU, also known as Kerkyra (and, in earlier times, variously as Corcyra, Scheria and Phaecia), is not the largest of the Ionian Islands, but it is the most populous, the most important and the most beautiful. It has suffered little from earthquakes, and was unaffected by that of 1953 which did so much damage elsewhere in the islands. The town, which unlike so many island capitals is indisputably a town, has an elegant Venetian core with British Neoclassical additions and at least one notable French one: the most fashionable meeting spot for its café society is a reprise of the Rue de Rivoli in Paris.

Its villages, however, were largely bypassed by such sophistications. Road communications were poor until the British arrived. The Venetian aristocracy built some memorable country houses but generally seems to have preferred life in town or back in Venice.

Corfiot villages developed in a more haphazard way than those in the rest of Greece. Land was plentiful and relatively unmountainous, so building space was not at a premium. Nor was attack the constant threat it was for other Greeks. Corfiot and other Ionian villages are less inclined to huddle tight around a *plateia* than villages elsewhere in Greece, indeed there rarely is a *plateia*. Instead, many spread out along or more precisely back from a road. One consequence is that they do not reveal themselves in the way that the classic Greek village of, say, Pelion does, and may at first sight lack the gem-like quality of Cycladic ones. Instead of starting one's explorations at (or even confining them to) the *plateia* and then moving out, you need to leave the main road and plunge into a Corfiot village. Gastouri and Ag Markos are prime examples of this. And where are their centres? It is impossible to say.

Gastouri is one of the few villages which has always had good communications with the town, both by land and by sea (to which it is close but from which it is invisible). The coast here, to the south of Corfu town, is also the first spot in Greece on which foreign eyes alighted when the mode for seaside holidays gathered momentum in the 19th century. The British headed for the Côte d'Azur, but central European monarchs, for whom Trieste was the gateway to the Mediterranean, came here. And in Gastouri you can see why. The similarities with the Riviera are striking, the same and in any other context quite un-Greek coastal combination of lushness with heat, as roses grow alongside olives and palms and the surounding hills contrive to be at once near-sheer in places yet abundantly treed.

The Empress Elizabeth of Austria built her summer palace, the Achilleion, here on what she perceived as a heroic Greek theme atop the ridge between Gastouri and the sea. Kaiser Wilhelm II subsequently acquired it, modestly added the incription, 'To the greatest of the Greeks from the greatest of the Germans,' to the statue of Achilles, and spent every spring here from 1908 until he got the war he wanted in 1914. Today, it is a casino. But drive up the main road towards this, past the mainly modern villas which herald its approach, and you will miss the village entirely. For this, you must head down side streets instead.

Because of its almost suburban relationship with the town, Gastouri has some Neoclassical urban influences such as arched ground floors, particularly where there are shops and cafés. These can be seen in other villages also, a reflection of the relative sophistication of Corfu.

Gastouri embraces the gamut of Ionian style. The big difference between the Ionian and the Aegean is that woodwork tends to be green (rather than blue) and walls ochre or terracotta (rather than white). Nobody quite knows the reason for the green; perhaps it is a reflection of the verdant landscape, but certainly there were never the revolutionary pressures in the Ionian which led to the use of blue for covert nationalistic reasons in Ottoman Greece. The traditional Ionian shutter is like those of Venice and Provence, being of solid wood rather than louvred, again unlike much of the rest of Greece. Though louvres are becoming the norm in modern houses.

Other characteristics include the symmetrical tendency of the houses, with a window on either side of a door, unless there is some overriding reason as to why there should not be, solid stone lintels on all four sides of the windows, gabled (rather than four-square or flat) roofs, and a covered porch or verandah. The latter encompasses two strong Corfiot features. The *botzos* is an outside structure, usually with an L-shaped staircase which goes up over a vaulted ground-floor entrance (where animals or agricultural implements would have been housed) ending at the porch outside the upstairs living quarters. The *ksehito* is a form of lean-to loggia with a tiled roof, sometimes on houses, nearly always outside olive presses, creating a shelter from sun and rain where produce may be loaded, unloaded or stored.

Corfu has perhaps the lushest landscape of all the Greek islands; olive and cypress predominate near the village of Spartilas (right).

*A*gios Markos was a dying village a generation ago. Now it is almost entirely foreign-occupied and renovated, as this house (opposite), which has retained an appealing sense of gentle decay. Gastouri (this page) was perhaps the first village in Greece to benefit from tourism, when it found favour with central European monarchs in the late 19th century.

*I*onian villages tend not to have central squares. Strinilas, halfway up Corfu's highest mountain (opposite), is one of the few exceptions. This millstone would have been used to press olives until recently and certainly within the lifetime of these ladies at Strinilas (this page) who, like many of their generation, still wear traditional Corfiot peasant clothes.

Paxos

THE UNUSUAL THING about the villages on Paxos (also known as Paxoi) is that most of them are not villages at all, but what translates roughly from the Greek as 'neighbourhoods'. These deconstruct one step further than the villages on Corfu, of which Paxos has traditionally been a dependency, in that not only do these have no square, central or otherwise, but most have no shops or cafés either, though they are more likely to have a church if not in the village itself then certainly close by and perhaps shared with other neighbourhoods, though less reverent Paxiots are wont to complain that they have more priests than they do doctors.

A further distinctively Paxiot feature is that most of these neighbourhoods bear the names of local families, thus Aronatika, Vassilatika, Tsenembesatika, etc. after the families (Aronis, Vassilas and Tsenembesis) who founded them. Though subsequent population movements, mostly through marriage, mean that a person's name is no longer a sure indication as to whereabouts they will live on Paxos.

Paxos appears to have been lightly populated throughout its history; it has but one unreliable natural water source, there is no record that it was inhabited at all in antiquity, though the Venetians took sufficient interest in it to cover almost the entire island with some of the most beautiful olive groves on earth, producing perhaps the finest oil in Greece. Most of today's families trace their origins back to the exodus from Parga on the mainland opposite in 1814 when the British declined to include the enclave in their Ionian protectorate and sold it to the Turks.

The little harbour of Longos (right), perhaps because it does not make for good yacht mooring, is one of the most perfect spots in the Ionian for the ritual of the waterside taverna meal.

*C*hurches of Paxos (opposite above left)*: behind and incorporated into the tiny church of Pantocrator in Makratika are the remains of what was once the private chapel of a Venetian great house. The church of Fontana, the largest inland village (opposite above right), has a notable September festival. And human comradeship is still alive and well on Paxos (opposite below).* Fine buildings, like this gate (above) of a ruined factory in Longos which once produced soap from olives, co-exist with purely touristic enterprises (left).

*O*live trees and cypresses dominate the Paxiot landscape (right): planting of the former was encouraged on a bounty system by the Venetians in the Middle Ages. According to some observers, the natural spread of the cypress south down the Ionian took place as recently as this century. The mountains of the Epiros on the mainland opposite will be snow-capped in winter.

Lefkas

Agias Nikitas (these pages), nestling in a ravine by the sea, is one of the few villages on Lefkas' wilder western shore and certainly the most attractive. Its picket fences (above) are among the features which can give the island a strangely Caribbean air.

ALSO KNOWN AS Leukas, Santa Mavra, Santa Maura, and most commonly in modern Greek Lefkada, Lefkas has had a mixed career as an island, with the shifting forces of man and nature making and breaking its tenuous link with the mainland over the centuries. The first ship canal to make an island of it was was built by Corinthians around 700 B.C., linking the open sea to the north with the sheltered waters first of a shallow lagoon and then of the inland sea created in the lee of Lefkas and Ithaca to the south. The point was not so much to create a short cut as a welcome respite from open seas for navigators between Corfu and Corinth.

This canal has gone through a cycle of silting up and enlargment ever since. It has also sometimes been bridged, but Lefkas today remains technically an island, a status which carries perceived political and fiscal advantage. The floating bridge which now permanently links it to the mainland (save when opening for passing yachts) has been cannily declared the ferry-boat *Santa Mavra*, and the man in charge its captain.

The island's names too have their paradoxes. Lefkas comes from the ancient Greek for white, in honour of its towering white southernmost cliffs from which the poetess Sappho leaped to her death, a spine-tingling spot. But then *mavra* is Greek for black. And Santa Mavra was the name the Venetians gave to the chapel in the fort they built beside the canal to secure the isthmus from land attack, and by extension this came to refer first to the fort itself and then the entire island.

Lefkas has other oddities. While the rest of the Ionian remained solidly Venetian, it passed back and forth between east and west, enduring some 200 years in all of Turkish occupation. It is notably less Italianate than the other islands but one of its most striking features seems to have been bequeathed by the Victorian British: that of building upper storeys of corrugated iron.

Lefkas is particularly prone to earthquakes and while the idea of building upper floors of light material (such as cadmus reed daubed with plaster) which was less likely to collapse than masonry, and less likely to injure if it should, was not new, that of using corrugated iron was. The British, who had used it to good effect in their tropical colonies, apparently gave the Lefkadians the idea. It worked well but caught on nowhere else. The often misty and reed-lined lagoon has a vaguely Oriental air.

The end of countless odysseys: Ithacans are great travellers and compulsive returnees, dreaming of a house, some vines and perhaps a small boat on the island they left behind (this page and opposite).

Ithaca

ITHACA, more celebrated in poetry than in life; one would imagine we could at least agree that it was the kingdom and eternal goal of Odysseus (after all, Homer is unequivocal on the point). Well, maybe, but Dörpfeld, the second most eminent German nineteenth-century archaeologist after Schliemann (he of Troy, who had dug in vain in Ithaca), devoted much time, energy and money to the theory that ancient Ithaca was really next-door Lefkas. No conclusive archaeological link between Ithaca (or anywhere else) and Homer's hero has ever been found, but there is no real reason to doubt that today's Ithaca and Homer's were one, and doubters and believers alike may enjoy attempting to retrace the last few miles of the *Odyssey*, book in hand.

The least unlikely site of Odysseus' 'palace' is near the village of Stavros, in the north of the island, where one candidate is not very helpfully (but accurately) signposted, 'Ancient city (sank)'. It has long seemed to me that this stretch of water, where shipping routes and islands meet between Ithaca's northern point, Sappho's leap on Lefkas opposite and nearby Kefallonia, is in a sense the nautical navel (*omphalos*) of Greece, just as Delphi was the terrestrial one, and that the Homeric and subsequent equations of Ithaca with the end of all our wandering might be more than an accident of history. The second most famous invocation of the island, this time a modern Greek poem, *Ithaca* by Cavafy, is a haunting icon for all our odysseys.

The Ithacans are ever wanderers (and returnees) and the island today, lacking airport and beaches, has not been entirely pulled back from depopulation by tourism. Besides, its wealthy if not famous sons wish to return from Boston, London, Johannesburg and Melbourne to something resembling the island they left behind. The man in the Stavros café who looks like a typical Greek villager is just as likely to prove a cultivated Londoner or a breezy Aussie. Ithaca retains a sparse dignity, a meeting of rock and sea and long-lost friends rather than a place of plenty.

*T*he fourteenth-century village church of Kimisi Theotokou (opposite and above) in Anogi has survived centuries of buffeting by the elements and earthquake on the high windsept uplands of Ithaca. Its stern Byzantine frescoes are fading now, but its outer fabric, seen here at the southern door, holds firm.

*D*etail and vista in Ithaca: the architectural detailing of a distant church and the proud maintenance of a small house (this page) *are sharp contrasts to the dramatic rise and fall of the island's stunning landscape* (right).

Kefallonia

THE LARGEST of the Ionian islands, with easily the highest mountain, Mount Enos, and its own species of fir tree (*Abies cephaloniensis*), it almost certainly formed part of Odysseus' kingdom and was much wrangled over by Crusaders. Its most attractive village, Fiskardon, is a corruption of the Norman name Guiscard (Robert Guiscard died here in 1085). Alas, Fiskardon is virtually all that remains of pre-earthquake Kefallonia, though Metaxata, where Byron lived for a year, retains a certain charm, with its hillside sea views across to the mainland from which he awaited the call to join the gathering liberation struggle. The house itself was a casualty of the 1953 earthquake.

The Kefallonians, who make some of the best wine in the Ionian, are a spirited and independent people, who excel in scholarship, soldiering, law, business and, most famously, in saying 'No'. The otherwise little lamented Greek dictator, General Metaxas, was of Kefallonian origin and allegedly dismissed a pompous and rambling ultimatum from Mussolini with just that utterance one day in 1940. That day, 28 October, is now hallowed as 'Oxi' ('No') day throughout Greece. The islanders also appear to have been the only Ionians to have rebelled against the British. Sir Charles Napier (the conqueror of Sind and author of another memorable and possibly apocryphal military one-worder: 'Peccavi') repaid the compliment by describing the Greeks he was governing here as 'worth all the other nations put together.'

Kefallonia today, shaken and sadly deforested (though the mighty firs on Mount Enos now enjoy belated protection), does not present an immediately alluring face to the visitor. Only Fiskardon, with its small harbour as almost the sole reminder of the island's former glory, shows a single-minded obsession with the tourist drachma, which it gouges with smiling efficiency from passing yachts.

Assos is in a picture-postcard setting at the mainland end of a narrow isthmus leading to a natural defensive site dominated by a Venetian fortress. One early British traveller, Leake, refers to Hellenic walls here. But there is no sign of these today. Edward Lear called the view from this fortress 'one of the sublimest scenes in the Seven Islands'. But the village below, partly reconstructed after the earthquake, is oddly insubstantial.

*A*ssos (right) *has regained a measure of its charm after a devastating earthquake with restoration funds from the city of Paris.*

*F*iskardon (this page) *is the only village on Kefallonia to have emerged virtually unscathed from the devastating 1953 earthquake; with its attractive back streets it is a popular port of call with land-based tourists, rivalling the attraction of the harbour of Assos* (opposite).

Overleaf
*E*dward Lear described the *view from the sixteenth-century Venetian fortress on the classic defensive site above Assos as 'one of the sublimest scenes in the Seven Islands'. Today, however, it is the view from the road at the other end of the isthmus as it descends to the village which has become an iconic symbol of Ionian beauty.*

Bibliography

ANDREWS, Kevin, *The Flight of Ikaros. A Journey in Greece*, London, 1959

APOLLONIUS OF RHODES, *The Voyage of Argo*, London, 1959

BARBER, Robin, *Greece, The Blue Guide*, London, 1995

BAUMANN, Helmut, *Greek Wildflowers and Plant Lore in Ancient Greece*, London, 1993

BENT, James, *The Cyclades, or Life among the Insular Greeks*, London, 1881

BOARDMAN, John, *Greek Art*, London, 1973

BRADFORD, Ernle, *The Companion Guide to the Greek Islands*, London, 1988

BURNIE, David, *Wild Flowers of the Mediterranean*, London, 1995

CALASSO, Roberto, *The Marriage of Cadmus and Harmony*, London, 1993

CAVAFY, C.P., *Collected Poems of C.P. Cavafy*, London, 1978

CHARLEMONT Lord, *Travels in Greece and Turkey 1749*, London, 1984

DURRELL, Gerald, *My Family and Other Animals*, London, 1956

DURRELL, Lawrence, *The Greek Islands*, London, 1978

DURRELL, Lawrence, *Prospero's Cell*, London, 1945

ELLINGHAM, Mark (ed.), *The Rough Guide to Greece*, London, 1995 (6th edition)

FERMOR, Patrick Leigh, *Mani, Travels in the Southern Peloponnese*, London, 1958

FERMOR, Patrick Leigh, *Roumeli, Travels in Northern Greece*, London, 1966

FOX, Robin Lane, *Alexander the Great*, London, 1973

GARRETT, Martin, *Greece, a Literary Companion*, London, 1994

GRAVES, Robert, *The Greek Myths*, London, 1958

GREEN, Peter, *From Alexander to Actium*, London, 1990

HERODOTUS, *The Histories*, London, 1954

HOMER, *The Iliad*, many editions

HOMER, *The Odyssey*, many editions

DE JONGH, Brian, *The Companion Guide to Mainland Greece*, London, 1979

KAZANTZAKIS, Nikos, *Travels in Greece – Journey to the Morea*, Oxford, 1966

KEELEY, Edmund and SHERRARD, Philip (trs.), *The Dark Crystal, An Anthology of Modern Greek Poetry by Cavafy, Sikelianos, Seferis, Elytis, Gatsos*, Athens, *c.* 1981

KERÉNY, Károly, *The Gods of the Greeks*, London, 1951

LEAKE, William, *Travels in Northern Greece* (4 volumes), London, 1835

LEAR, Edward, *Edward Lear in Greece*, London, 1965

LEVI, Peter, *The Hill of Kronos*, London, 1991

MAZOWER, Mark, *Inside Hitler's Greece*, Yale, 1995

MICHELIN GUIDE, *Greece*, Watford, 1995

MILLER, Henry, *The Colossus of Maroussi*, London, 1942

NORWICH, John Julius, *The Byzantine Trilogy*, London, 1996

PAUSANIUS, *Guide to Greece* (2 volumes), London, 1979

PHILLIPIDES, Dimitri (ed.), *Greek Traditional Architecture* (Volumes 1 and 2 available in English), Athens, *c.* 1983

POFFLEY, Frewin, *Greek Island Hopping*, London, annually

POWELL, Elizabeth Dilys, *An Affair of the Heart*, London, 1958

POWELL, Elizabeth Dilys, *The Villa Ariadne*, London, 1973

SEVERIN, Tim, *The Ulysses Voyage, Sea Search for the Odyssey*, London, 1987

SLESIN, Suzanne et al., *Greek Style*, London, 1988

SPIVEY, Nigel, *Understanding Greek Sculpture*, London, 1996

THUCYDIDES *The Peloponnesian War*, London, 1954

WOODHOUSE, Christopher Montague, *The Story of Modern Greece*, London, 1968

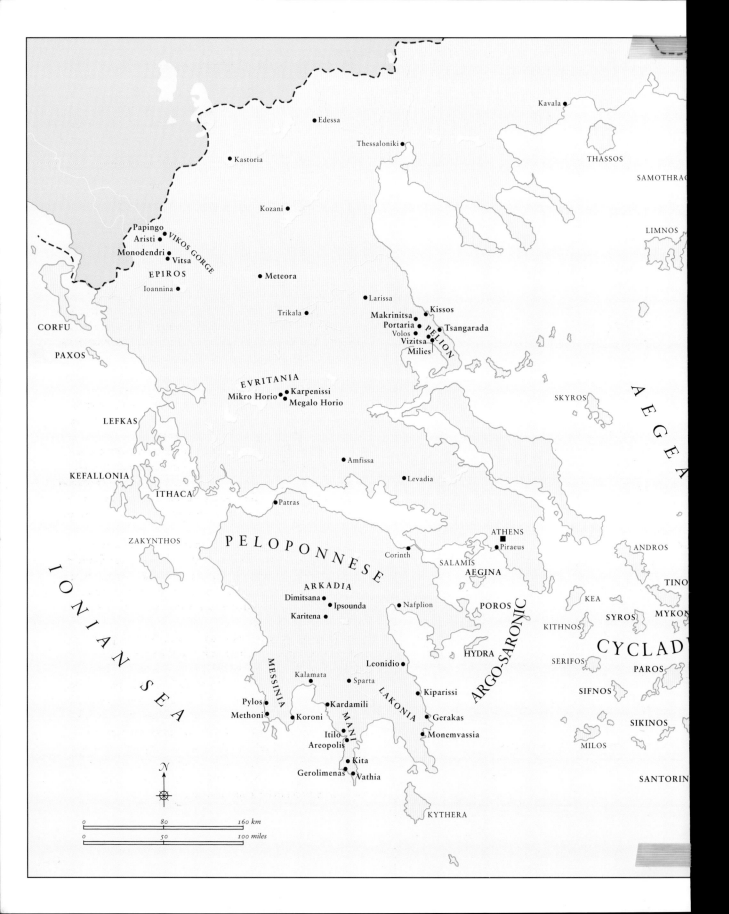

Kavala

THASSOS

SAMOTHRAC

Edessa

Thessaloniki

Kastoria

LIMNOS

Kozani

Papingo

Aristi

VIKOS GORGE

Monodendri

Vitsa

EPIROS

Meteora

Ioannina

Larissa

Kissos

Makrinitsa

Portaria

Tsangarada

Volos

PELION

Vizitsa

Milies

CORFU

PAXOS

EVRITANIA

Karpenissi

Mikro Horio

Megalo Horio

SKYROS

A E G E A

LEFKAS

KEFALLONIA

Amfissa

ITHACA

Levadia

Patras

ATHENS

ANDROS

ZAKYNTHOS

PELOPONNESE

Corinth

Piraeus

SALAMIS

AEGINA

TINO

ARKADIA

Dimitsana

Ipsounda

Nafplion

POROS

KEA

MYKON

Karitena

KITHNOS

SYROS

CYCLAD

HYDRA

SERIFOS

PAROS

Leonidio

ARGO-SARONIC

MESSINIA

Kalamata

Sparta

SIFNOS

Pylos

Kiparissi

LAKONIA

SIKINOS

Methoni

Kardamili

Gerakas

Koroni

MANI

Itilo

Monemvassia

MILOS

Areopolis

Kita

SANTORIN

Gerolimenas

Vathia

KYTHERA

N

0   80   160 km

0   50   100 miles

IONIAN SEA

The Transliteration of Place Names

The Greek alphabet is older than and an immediate ancestor of our own Roman alphabet. It has 24 letters and although it can have several ways of rendering some sounds (notably the long 'e') Greek is much more precise than English when read. Thus, in any given context there can only be one way to pronounce any letter or diphthong and thus a word. However, this will bear little if any resemblance to the pronunciation beloved of classicists.

The transliteration of Greek into the Roman alphabet has fewer certainties, not least because, unlike the Greek, the latter is used by many different languages which often pronounce the same Roman letters in different ways. In the transliteration of Greek into English, consistency and common sense are what are mainly called for. Some illogicalities, however, are inevitable and indeed desirable due to custom and practice. Thus, although it might seem pedantic, imprecise, and contrary to common-sense to change a Greek letter 'k' that both exists in and is pronounced exactly the same in the Roman alphabet into the letter 'c', a letter that exists only in the Roman alphabet where it can be pronounced quite differently, I suspect we are forever saddled with Ithaca and the Cyclades Islands because several centuries ago that was how they were arbitrarily rendered.

Similarly, changing familiar place names such as Athens to 'Athinai' merely defeats the purpose of language and spelling, which is to convey information with the minimum of confusion. Unfortunately there is the added complication that the Greeks themselves may have more than one name or version of a name for a place.

Where more than one name or transliteration of a place name exists then I have endeavoured to give the more familiar version plus any common alternatives. Only one practice when rendering names from Greek seems to me thoroughly perverse and wrong-headed, and that is their Latinization, as when 'Epiros' becomes 'Epirus'.

It is, however, worth mentioning in a book about places that the Greek *gamma* behaves much as the letter 'g' does with us, being soft (sounding like our 'y') before 'e' and 'i', hard elsewhere. Thus the Greek for 'saint' in which the second letter is *gamma* is sensibly rendered as 'ayios' rather than 'agios', with 'aghios' as an occasional compromise. However, this common prefix to many place names is often shortened on maps and signposts in both Greek and Roman alphabets to the first two letters of the word (just as 'Saint' becomes 'St'). Conventionally, and misleadingly, this is rendered into the Roman as 'Ag', but this convention has been retained here.

Author's Acknowledgements

Without the Greeks themselves this book would not be.
Thanks are due to: especially Manos Anglias, one-time *hôtelier*
supreme (and now new Australian), Babis Hadjimikaelis, the
eminent Corfiot architect, and Spyros Lychnos, also of Corfu,
my first Greek friend and with whom it all began.
In London, Dr. Nikos Papadakis of the Greek Embassy,
the staff at the National Tourist Office of Greece, and Irene and
Stamos J. Fafalios were all generous with their time, libraries
and knowledge, while without the encouragement of Christine
Walker, Travel Editor of the *Sunday Times*, I would know much
less about the country than I do today. This book also owes a
debt of gratitude to David Watrous of the Greek Islands Club,
without whom Hugh Palmer and I would have never met.
Clovis Keath has been my constant other half and other eyes
in discovering Greece from the start. The text of this
book, and its author, owe most to her.

Photographer's Acknowledgments

The photographs in this book are dedicated to my tireless
travelling companions: Janet Hales, Vicky Taylor and Kath
McPhail. The unpredictability of travelling in Greece is part of
its charm: the frustrations that sometimes result are always
made up for by the warmth and generosity of its people. From
countless encounters with kind friends, I should like to thank
especially: Tula Koronios, Marianna Vidalis, Bill Parais,
Pano Aronis, Iannis Georkidakis and Anthe
and Anastasis Karaginnis.